Owned by Several Masters

By
Sojourner Truth

PADMORE PUBLISHING GROUP

Owned by Several Masters Editing, Research and Additional Writing: Angela Mosley © 2016 All rights reserved. Printed in the United States of America. No part of this publication may be reproduced, adapted or transmitted in any form or by any means, electronic or mechanical, including photocopy, recording, or any information storage and retrieval system, without permission in writing from the publisher. For more information, please go to: www.padmorepublishing.com

Cover design: Viveca Batiste
© Cover: Padmore Publishing Group
Library of Congress cataloging in publication data
ISBN: 978-1-939866-07-3 (paperback)

By
Sojourner Truth

PADMORE BOOKS   OWNED BY SEVERAL MASTERS

Editor's preface

The following is the unpretending narrative of the life of a remarkable and meritorious woman–a life which has been checkered by strange vicissitudes, severe hardships, and singular adventures. Born a slave, and held in that brutal condition until the entire abolition of slavery in the State of New York in 1827, she has known what it is to drink to the dregs the bitterest cup of human degradation. That one thus placed on a level with cattle and swine, and for so many years subjected to the most demoralizing influences, should have retained her moral integrity to such an extent, and cherished so successfully the religious sentiment in her soul, shows a mind of no common order.

This story is written in the vernacular of the time - the original narrative was written by the editor of the publishing house who bought the rights of her story based on her oral accounts of her trials and tribulations. Since Sojourner, (originally named Isabella by her master), remained unable to read or write her whole life, she relied on a friend, Olive Gilbert, to retell her story from her own oral recount of her life and experience as a slave and as a lecturer in churches in the north-east were she offered her testimony. Gilbert injected quite a bit of her own commentary on both Truth and the abolitionist movement on the first edition of her story called Narrative of a Northern Slave, making it hard for readers to follow the narrative due to all the interjections.

This new version, Owned by Several Masters, dismisses the third person narrator and puts the narrating spotlight on the one who could tell us as if she was in the same room with us. In this more linear narration, the story of this brave woman is more intertwined. The mission of this new version is to capture the strength of Sojourner's voice, so that her optimism, spirit, and determination shines throughout her narrative. Also, it is for young readers to feel that she is talking directly to them, asking them to think about the injustices she, and others like her, suffered.

"SWEET is the virgin honey,
though the wild bee store it in a reed;
And bright the jeweled band
that circleth an Ethiop's arm;
Pure are the grains of gold
in the turbid stream of the Ganges;
And fair the living flowers
that spring from the dull cold sod.
Wherefore, thou gentle student,
bend thine ear to my speech,
For I also am as thou art;
our hearts can commune together:
To meanest matters will I stoop,
for mean is the lot of mortal;
I will rise to noblest themes,
for the soul hath a heritage of glory."

My birth and parentage

I, SOJOURNER TRUTH, as I now call myself–but whose name, originally, was Isabella–was born, as near as I can now calculate, between the years 1797 and 1800. I was the daughter of James and Betsey, slaves of Colonel Ardinburgh, of Hurley, Ulster County, New York. Colonel Ardinburgh belonged to that class of people called Low Dutch.

Of my first master, I can give no account, as I must have been a mere infant when he died; and I, with my parents and some ten or twelve other fellow human slaves, became the legal property of his son, Charles Ardinburgh. I distinctly remember hearing my father and mother say, that their lot was a fortunate one, as Master Charles was the best of the family,–being, comparatively speaking, a kind master to his slaves.

James and Betsey having, by their faithfulness, docility, and respectful behavior, won his particular regard, received from him particular favors–among which was a lot of land, lying back on the slope of a mountain, where, by improving it on the pleasant evenings and Sundays, they managed to raise a little tobacco, corn, or flax; which they exchanged for extras, in the articles of food or clothing for themselves and children.

Accommodations

Among my earliest recollections was the removal of my master, Charles Ardinburgh, into his new house, which he had built for a hotel, soon after the decease of his father. A cellar, under this hotel, was assigned to his slaves, as their sleeping apartment,–all the slaves he possessed, of both sexes, sleeping (as is quite common in a state of slavery) in the same room. I carry in my mind, to this day, a vivid picture of this dismal chamber; its only lights consisting of a few panes of glass, through which the sun never shone, but with thrice reflected rays; and the space between the loose boards of the floor, and the uneven earth below, was often filled with mud and water, the uncomfortable splashings of which were as annoying as its noxious vapors must have been chilling and fatal to health.

I shudder, even now, as I go back in memory, and revisit this cellar, and see its inmates, of both sexes and all ages, sleeping on those damp boards, like the horse, with a little straw and a blanket; and I wonder not at the rheumatisms, and fever-sores, and palsies, that distorted the limbs and racked the bodies of those fellow-slaves in after-life. Still, I do not attribute this cruelty–for cruelty it certainly is, to be so unmindful of the health and comfort of any being, leaving entirely out of sight his more important part, his everlasting interests,–so much to any innate or constitutional cruelty of the master, as to that gigantic inconsistency, that inherited habit among slaveholders, of expecting a willing and intelligent obedience from the slave, because he is a MAN–at the same time everything belonging to the soul-harrowing system does its best to crush the last vestige of a man within him; and when it is crushed, and often before, he is denied the comforts of life, on the plea that he knows neither the want nor the use of them, and because he is considered to be little more or little less than a beast.

My brothers and sisters

My father was very tall and straight, when young, which gave him the name of 'Bomefree'–low Dutch for tree–and by this name he usually went. The most familiar appellation of my mother was 'Mau-mau Bett.' She was the mother of some ten or twelve children; though I'm far from knowing the exact number of my brothers and sisters; I being the youngest, save one, and all older than myself having been sold before I could meet them. I had the privilege to behold six of them while I remained a slave.

Of the two that immediately preceded me in age, a boy of five years, and a girl of three, who were sold when I was an infant, I heard much; and I wished that all who would fain believe that slave parents have not natural affection for their offspring could have listened as I did, while Bomefree and Mau-mau Bett,–their dark cellar lighted by a blazing pine-knot,–would sit for hours, recalling and recounting every endearing, as well as harrowing circumstance that taxed memory could supply, from the histories of those dear departed ones, of whom they had been robbed, and for whom their hearts still bled.

Among the stories, they would relate how one of their little boys, on the last morning he was with them, arose with the birds, kindled a fire, calling for his Mau-mau to 'come, for all was now ready for her'–little dreaming of the dreadful separation which was so near at hand, but of which his parents had an uncertain, but all the more cruel foreboding. There was snow on the ground, at the time of which we are speaking; and a large old-fashioned sleigh was seen to drive up to the door of the late Col. Ardinburgh. This event was noticed with childish pleasure by the unsuspicious boy; but when he was taken and put into the sleigh, and saw his little sister actually shut and locked into the sleigh box, his eyes were at once opened to their intentions; and, like a frightened deer he sprang from the sleigh, and running into the house, concealed himself under a bed. But this availed him little. He was reconvened to the sleigh, and separated forever from those whom God had constituted his natural guardians and protectors.

My religious instruction

Peter, my youngest brother, and I remained, with our parents, the legal property of Charles Ardinburgh till his decease, which took place when I was near nine years old.

After this event, I was often surprised to find my mother in tears; and when, in my simplicity, I inquired, 'Mau-mau, what makes you cry?' she would answer, 'Oh, my child, I am thinking of your brothers and sisters that have been sold away from me.' And she would proceed to detail many circumstances respecting them. But I have long since concluded that it was the impending fate of her only remaining children, which my mother but too well understood, even then, that called up those memories from the past, and made them crucify her heart afresh.

In the evening, when my mother's work was done, she would sit down under the sparkling vault of heaven, and calling her children to her, would talk to us of the only Being that could effectually aid or protect us. Her teachings were delivered in Low Dutch, her only language, and, translated into English, ran nearly as follows:–

'My children, there is a God, who hears and sees you.'
'A God, Mau-mau! Where does he live?' asked us children.
'He lives in the sky,' she replied; 'and when you are beaten, or cruelly treated, or fall into any trouble, you must ask help of him, and he will always hear and help you.'

She taught us to kneel and say the Lord's Prayer. She entreated us to refrain from lying and stealing, and to strive to obey our masters.

At times, a groan would escape her, and she would break out in the language of the Psalmist–
'Oh Lord, how long?' 'Oh Lord, how long?' And in reply to my question–'What ails you, Mau-mau?' her

only answer was, 'Oh, a good deal ails me'–'Enough ails me.' Then again, she would point us to the stars, and say, in her peculiar language, 'Those are the same stars, and that is the same moon, that look down upon your brothers and sisters, and which they see as they look up to them, though they are ever so far away from us, and each other.'

Thus, in her humble way, she did endeavor to show us our Heavenly Father, as the only being who could protect us in our perilous condition; at the same time, she would strengthen and brighten the chain of family affection, which she trusted extended itself sufficiently to connect the widely scattered members of her precious flock. These instructions from my mother I treasured up and held sacred for all my life.

The auction

At length, the never-to-be-forgotten day of the terrible auction arrived, when the 'slaves, horses, and other cattle' of Charles Ardinburgh, deceased, were to be put under the hammer, and again change masters. Not only Peter and me, but our mother, were now destined to the auction block, and would have been struck off with the rest to the highest bidder, but for the following circumstance:

A question arose among the heirs, 'Who shall be burdened with Bomefree, when we have sent away his faithful Mau-mau Bett?'
He was becoming weak and infirm; his limbs were painfully rheumatic and distorted–more from exposure and hardship than from old age, though he was several years older than Mau-mau Bett: he was no longer considered of value, but must soon be a burden and care to someone.

After some contention on the point at issue, none being willing to be burdened with him, it was finally agreed, as most expedient for the heirs, that the price of Mau-mau Bett should be sacrificed, and she receive her freedom, on condition that she takes care of and support her faithful James,–faithful, not only to her as a husband, but proverbially faithful as a slave to those who would not willingly sacrifice a dollar for his comfort, now that he had commenced his descent into the dark valley of decrepitude and suffering.

This important decision was received as joyful news indeed by the ancient couple, who were the objects of it, and who were trying to prepare their hearts for a severe struggle, and one altogether new to them, as they had never before been separated; for, though ignorant, helpless, crushed in spirit, and weighed down with hardship and cruel bereavement, they were still human, and their human hearts beat within them with as true an affection as ever caused a human heart to beat. And their anticipated separation now, in the decline of life, after the last child had been torn from them, must have been truly appalling.

Another privilege was granted to them –that of remaining occupants of the same dark, humid cellar I have before described: otherwise, they were to support themselves as they best could. And as my mother was still able to do considerable work, and my father a little, they got on for some time very comfortably. The strangers who rented the house were humane people, and very kind to them; they were not rich, and owned no slaves. How long this state of things continued, I'm unable to say, as I had not then sufficiently cultivated my studies to calculate years, or even weeks or hours. But I think my mother must have lived several years after the death of Master Charles. I remember going to visit my parents some three or four times before the death of my mother, and a good deal of time seemed to intervene between each visit.

At length my mother's health began to decline–a fever-sore made its ravages on one of her limbs, and the palsy began to shake her frame; still, she and James tottered about, picking up a little here and there, which, added to the mites contributed by their kind neighbors, sufficed to sustain life, and drive famine from the door.

Death of Mau-mau Bett

One morning, in early autumn, (from the reason above mentioned, I cannot tell what year,) Mau-mau Bett told James she would make him a loaf of rye-bread, and get Mrs. Simmons, their kind neighbor, to bake it for them, as she would bake that forenoon. James told her he had engaged to rake after the cart for his neighbors that morning; but before he commenced, he would pole off some apples from a tree near, which they were allowed to gather; and if she could get some of them baked with the bread, it would give a nice relish for their dinner. He beat off the apples, and soon after, saw Mau-mau Bett come out and gather them up.

At the blowing of the horn for dinner, he groped his way into his cellar, anticipating his humble, but warm and nourishing meal; when, lo! instead of being cheered by the sight and odor of fresh-baked bread and the savory apples, his cellar seemed more cheerless than usual, and at first neither sight nor sound met eye or ear. But, on groping his way through the room, his staff, which he used as a pioneer to go before, and warn him of danger, seemed to be impeded in its progress, and a low, gurgling, choking sound proceeded from the object before him, giving him the first intimation of the truth as it was, that Mau-mau Bett, his bosom companion, the only remaining member of his large family, had fallen in a fit of the palsy, and lay helpless and senseless on the earth!

Who among us, located in pleasant homes, surrounded with every comfort, and so many kind and sympathizing friends, can picture ourselves in the dark and desolate state of poor old James– penniless, weak, lame, and nearly blind, as he was at the moment he found his companion was removed from him, and he was left alone in the world, with no one to aid, comfort, or console him? for she never revived again, and lived only a few hours after being discovered senseless by her poor James.

Last days of Bomefree

I was permitted, along with Peter, to see the remains of our mother as she laid in her last narrow dwelling, and to make our bereaved father a little visit, before we were returned to our servitude. And most piteous were the lamentations of the poor old man, when, at last, we also were obliged to bid him 'Farewell!' Juan Fernandes, on his desolate island, was not so pitiable an object as this poor lame man. Blind and crippled, he was too superannuated to think for a moment of taking care of himself, and he greatly feared no persons would interest themselves in his behalf.

'Oh,' he would exclaim, 'I had thought God would take me first,–Mau-mau was so much smarter than I, and could get about and take care of herself;–and I am so old, and so helpless. What is to become of me? I can't do anything anymore–my children are all gone, and here I am left helpless and alone.' '

And then, as I was taking leave of him, he raised his voice, and cried aloud like a child–Oh, how he DID cry! I HEAR it now –and remember it as well as if it were but yesterday–poor old man!!! He thought God had done it all–and my heart bled within me at the sight of his misery. He begged me to get permission to come and see him sometimes, which I readily and heartily promised him.

But when all had left him, the Ardinburghs, having some feeling left for their faithful and favorite slave, 'took turns about' in keeping him–permitting him to stay a few weeks at one house, and then a while at another, and so around. If, when he had to move, the place where he was going was not too far off, he took up his line of march, staff in hand, and asked for no assistance. If it was twelve or twenty miles, they gave him a ride.

While he was living in this way, I was twice permitted to visit him. Years after, I even walked twelve miles, and carried my infant daughter in my arms, to see my father, but when I reached the place where I'd hoped to find him, he had just left for a place some twenty miles distant, and I never saw him again. The last time I did see him, I found him seated on a rock, by the roadside, alone, and far from any house. He was then migrating from the house of one Ardinburgh to that of another, several miles distant. His hair was white like wool–he was almost blind–and his gait was more a creep than a walk–but the weather was warm and pleasant, and he did not dislike the journey.

When I addressed him, he recognized my voice, and was exceeding glad to see me. He was assisted to mount the wagon, was carried back to the famous cellar of which we have spoken, and there we held our last earthly conversation. He again, as usual, bewailed his loneliness,–spoke in tones of anguish of his many children, saying, 'They are all taken away from me! I have now not one to give me a cup of cold water–why should I live and not die?'

My heart yearned over my father, and I would have made any sacrifice to have been able to be with him, and take care of him, tried to comfort, by telling him that I had heard the white folks say, that all the slaves in the State would be freed in ten years, and that then I would come and take care of him.

'I would take just as good care of you as Mau-mau would, if she was here'–I told him.
'Oh, my child,' replied he, 'I cannot live that long.'
'Oh, do, daddy, do live, and I will take such good care of you,' was my rejoinder.

Why, I thought then, in my ignorance, that he could live, if he just wished it. I just as much thought so, as I ever thought anything in my life–and I insisted on his living: but he shook his head, and insisted he could not.

I later learned that before Bomefree's good constitution would yield either to age, exposure, or a strong desire to die, the Ardinburghs again tired of him. They offered freedom to two old slaves– Caesar, brother of Mau-mau Bett, and his wife Betsey–on condition that they should take care of James. (I was about to say, 'their brother-in-law'–but as slaves are neither husbands nor wives in law, the idea of their being brothers-in-law is truly ludicrous.) And although they were too old and infirm to take care of themselves, (Cæsar having been afflicted for a long time with fever-sores, and his wife with the jaundice), they eagerly accepted the boon of freedom, which had been the life-long desire of their souls–though at a time when emancipation was to them little more than destitution, and was a freedom more to be desired by the master than the slave.

Death of Bomefree

A rude cabin, in a lone wood, far from any neighbors, was granted to our freed friends, as the only assistance they were now to expect. Bomefree, from this time, found his poor needs hardly supplied, as his new providers were scarcely able to administer to their own wants. However, the time drew near when things were to be decidedly worse rather than better; for they had not been together long, before Betty died, and shortly after, Caesar followed her to 'that bourne from whence no traveller returns'–leaving my poor father James again desolate, and more helpless than ever before; as, this time, there was no kind family in the house, and the Ardinburghs no longer invited him to their homes.

Yet, lone, blind and helpless as he was, James for a time lived on. One day, an aged colored woman, named Soan, called at his shanty, and James besought her, in the most moving manner, even with tears, to tarry awhile and wash and mend him up, so that he might once more be decent and comfortable; for he was suffering dreadfully with the filth and vermin that had collected upon him.

Soan was herself an emancipated slave, old and weak, with no one to care for her; and she lacked the courage to undertake a job of such seeming magnitude, fearing she might herself get sick, and perish there without assistance; and with great reluctance, and a heart swelling with pity, as she afterwards declared, she felt obliged to leave him in his wretchedness and filth. And shortly after her visit, this faithful slave, this deserted wreck of humanity, was found on his miserable pallet, frozen and stiff in death. The kind angel had come at last, and relieved him of the many miseries that his fellowman had heaped upon him. Yes, he had died, chilled and starved, with none to speak a kindly word, or do a kindly deed for him, in that last dread of hour of need!

The news of his death reached the ears of John Ardinburgh, a grandson of the old Colonel; and he declared that 'Bomefree, who had ever been a kind and faithful slave, should now have a good funeral.' And now, dear reader, what do you think constituted a good funeral? Answer–some black paint for the coffin, and a jug of ardent spirits! What a compensation for a life of toil, of patient submission to repeated robberies of the most aggravated kind, and, also, far more than murderous neglect!! Mankind often vainly attempts to atone for unkindness or cruelty to the living, by honoring the same after death; but John Ardinburgh undoubtebly meant his pot of paint and jug of whiskey should act as an opiate on his slaves, rather than on his own seared conscience.

My trials in life begin

Having seen the sad end of my parents, so far as it relates to this earthly life, I will return to my story at that memorable auction which threatened to separate me from my father and mother. A slave auction is a terrible affair to its victims, and its incidents and consequences are graven on their hearts as with a pen of burning steel.

At this memorable time, I was struck off, for the sum of one hundred dollars, to one John Nealy, of Ulster County, New York; and I have an impression that in this sale I was connected with a lot of sheep. I was now nine years of age, and my trials in life may be dated from this period. 'Now the war began.' I could only talk Dutch–and the Nealys could only talk English. Mr. Nealy could understand Dutch, but me and my mistress could neither understand the language of the other–and this, of itself, was a formidable obstacle in the way of a good understanding between us, and for some time was a fruitful source of dissatisfaction to the mistress, and of punishment and suffering to me. If they sent me for a frying pan, not knowing what they meant, perhaps I carried them pothooks and trammels. Then, oh! how angry mistress would be with me!

During the winter, I suffered terribly-terribly, with the cold. My feet were badly frozen, for want of proper covering. They gave me plenty to eat, and also plenty of whippings. One Sunday morning, in particular, I was told to go to the barn; on going there, I found my master with a bundle of rods, prepared in the embers, and bound together with cords. When he had tied my hands together before me, he gave me the most cruel whipping I was ever tortured with. He whipped me till the flesh was deeply lacerated, and the blood streamed from my wounds–and the scars remain to the present day, to testify to the fact. And now, when I hear them tell of whipping women on the bare flesh, it makes my flesh crawl, and my very hair rise on my head! Oh! my God! what a way is this of treating human beings?'

In those hours of my extremity, I did not forget the instructions of my mother, to go to God in all my trials, and every affliction; and I not only remembered, but obeyed: going to him, 'and telling him all–and asking Him if He thought it was right,' and begging him to protect and shield me from my persecutors.

I always asked with an unwavering faith that I should receive just what I pleaded for,– And now, though it seems curious, I do not remember ever asking for anything but what I got it. And I always received it as an answer to my prayers. When I got beaten, I never knew it long enough to go beforehand to pray; and I always thought that if I only had had time to pray to God for help, I should have escaped the beating.

I had no idea God had any knowledge of my thoughts, save what I told him; or heard my prayers, unless they were spoken audibly. And consequently, I could not pray unless I had time and opportunity to go by myself, where I could talk to God without being overheard.

Trials Continued

When I had been at Mr. Nealy's several months, I began to beg God most earnestly to send my father to me, and as soon as I commenced to pray, I began as confidently to look for his coming, and, it was not long, to my great joy, that he came. I had no opportunity to speak to him of the troubles that weighed so heavily on my spirit, while he remained; but when he left, I followed him to the gate, and unburdened my heart to him, inquiring if he could not do something to get me a new and better place. In this way the slaves often assist each other, by ascertaining who are kind to their slaves, comparatively; and then using their influence to get such one to hire or buy their friends; and masters, often from policy, as well as from latent humanity, allow those they are about to sell or let, to choose their own places, if the persons they happen to select for masters are considered safe pay. He promised to do all he could, and we parted. But, every day, as long as the snow lasted, (for there was snow on the ground at the time,) I returned to the spot where we separated, and walking in the tracks my father had made in the snow, repeated my prayer that 'God would help my father get me a new and better place.'

A long time had not elapsed, when a fisherman by the name of Scriver appeared at Mr. Nealy's, and inquired 'if I would like to go and live with him.' I eagerly answered 'Yes,' and nothing doubting but he was sent in answer to my prayer; and I soon started off with him, walking while he rode; for he had bought me at the suggestion of my father, paying one hundred and five dollars for me. He also lived in Ulster County, but some five or six miles from Mr. Nealy's.

Scriver, besides being a fisherman, kept a tavern for the accommodation of people of his own class–for his was a rude, uneducated family, exceedingly profane in their language, but, on the whole, an honest, kind and well-disposed people.

They owned a large farm, but left it wholly unimproved; attending mainly to their vocations of fishing and inn-keeping. I can ill describe the kind of life I led with them. It was a wild, out-of-door kind of life. I was expected to carry fish, to hoe corn, to bring roots and herbs from the woods for beers, go to the Strand for a gallon of molasses or liquor as the case might require, and 'browse around'. It was a life that suited me well for the time–being as devoid of hardship or terror as it was of improvement; a need which had not yet become a want. Instead of improving at this place, I retrograded, as their example taught me to curse; and it was here that I took my first oath.

After living with them for about a year and a half, I was sold to one John J. Dumont, for the sum of seventy pounds. This was in 1810. Mr. Dumont lived in the same county as my former masters, in the town of New Paltz, and I remained with him till a short time previous to my emancipation by the State, in 1828.

my new master and mistress

Had Mrs. Dumont possessed that vein of kindness and consideration for the slaves, so perceptible in her husband's character, I would have been as comfortable here, as one had best be, if one must be a slave. Mr. Dumont had been nursed in the very lap of slavery, and being naturally a man of kind feelings, treated his slaves with all the consideration he did his other animals, and more, perhaps.

But Mrs. Dumont, who had been born and educated in a non-slaveholding family, and, like many others, used only to work people, who, under the most stimulating of human motives, were willing to put forth their every energy, could not have patience with the creeping gait, the dull understanding, or see any cause for the listless manners and careless, slovenly habits of the poor down- trodden outcast– entirely forgetting that every high and efficient motive had been removed far from him; and that, had not his very intellect been crushed out of him, the slave would find little ground for aught but hopeless despondency.

From this source arose a long series of trials in my life, which I must pass over in silence; some from motives of delicacy, and others, because the relation of them might inflict undeserved pain on some now living, whom I remember only with esteem and love; therefore, the reader will not be surprised if my story appears somewhat tame at this point, and may rest assured that it is not for want of facts, as the most thrilling incidents of this portion of my life are from various motives suppressed.

One comparatively trifling incident I wish to relate, as it made a deep impression on my mind at the time–showing, as I think, how God shields the innocent, and causes them to triumph over their enemies, and also how I stood between master and mistress. In her family, Mrs. Dumont employed two white girls, one of whom, named Kate, evinced a disposition to 'lord it over' to me, and, 'to grind me down'. My master often shielded me from the attacks and accusations of others, praising me for my readiness and ability to work, and these praises seemed to foster a spirit of hostility toward me in the minds of Mrs. Dumont and her white servant, the latter of whom took every opportunity to cry up my faults, lessen me in the esteem of my master and increase against me the displeasure of my mistress, which was already more than sufficient for my comfort.

My master insisted that I could do as much work as half a dozen common people, and do it well, too; whilst my mistress insisted that the first was true, only because it ever came from her hand but half performed. A good deal of feeling arose from this difference of opinion, which was getting to rather an uncomfortable height, when, all at once, the potatoes that I cooked for breakfast assumed a dingy, dirty look. My mistress blamed me severely, asking my master to observe 'a fine specimen of Bell's work!'– adding, 'it is the way all her work is done.' My master scolded me also this time, and commanded me to be more careful in future. Kate joined with zest in the censures, and was very hard upon me. I thought that I had done all I could to do the potatoes good; and became quite distressed at their appearance, and wondered what I should do to avoid it.

In this dilemma, Gertrude Dumont (Mr. D.'s eldest child, a good, kind-hearted girl of ten years, who pitied me sincerely), when she heard them all blame me so unsparingly, came forward, offering her sympathy and assistance; and when about to retire to bed that night, she approached me, and told me, if I would wake her early next morning, she would get up and attend to the potatoes for me, while I went to milking, and they would see that the potatoes would come out nice, and not have 'Poppee,' her word for father, and 'Matty,' her word for mother, and all of 'em, scolding me so terribly.

I gladly availed herself of this kindness, which touched my heart, amid so much of an opposite spirit. When I had put the potatoes over to boil, Getty told me she would herself tend the fire, while I milked. She had not long been seated by the fire, in performance of her promise, when Kate entered, and requested Gertrude to go out of the room and do something for her, which she refused, still keeping her place in the corner. While there, Kate came sweeping about the fire, caught up a chip, lifted some ashes with it, and dashed them into the kettle. Now the mystery was solved, the plot discovered! Kate was working a little too fast at making her mistress's words good, at showing that Mrs. Dumont and herself were on the right side of the dispute, and consequently at gaining power over me. Yes, she was quite too fast, inasmuch as she had overlooked the little figure of justice, which sat in the corner, with scales nicely balanced, waiting to give all their dues.

But the time had come when she was to be overlooked no longer. It was Getty's turn to speak now. 'Oh Poppee! oh Pop- pee!' said she, 'Kate has been putting ashes in among the potatoes! I saw her do it! Look at those that fell on the outside of the kettle! You can now see what made the potatoes so dingy every morning, though Bell washed them clean!' And she repeated her story to every newcomer, till the fraud was made as public as the censure of me had been. My mistress looked blank, and remained dumb–my master muttered something which sounded very like an oath–and poor Kate was so chop-fallen, she looked like a convicted criminal, who would gladly have hidden herself, (now that the baseness was out,) to conceal her mortified pride and deep chagrin.

It was a fine triumph for me and my master, and I became more ambitious than ever to please him; and he stimulated my ambition by his commendation, and by boasting of me to his friends, telling them that I 'was better to me than a man–for she will do a good family's washing in the night, and be ready in the morning to go into the field, where she will do as much at raking and binding as my best hands.'

My ambition and desire to please were so great, that I often worked several nights in succession, sleeping only short snatches, as I sat in my chair; and some nights I would not allow myself to take any sleep, save what I could get resting myself against the wall, fearing that if I sat down, I would sleep too long. These extra exertions to please, and the praises consequent upon them, brought upon my head the envy of my fellow-slaves, and they taunted me with being the 'white folks' nigger.' On the other hand, I received the larger share of the confidence of my master, and many small favors that were by them unattainable. Someone asked me later if my master, Dumont, ever whipped me? And I answered, 'Oh yes, he sometimes whipped me soundly, though never cruelly. And the most severe whipping he ever gave me was because I was cruel to a cat.'

At this time I looked upon my master as a God; and believed that he knew of and could see me at all times, even as God himself. And I used sometimes to confess my delinquencies, from the conviction that he already knew them, and that I should fare better if I confessed them voluntarily: and if anyone talked to me of the injustice of me being a slave, I answered them with contempt, and immediately told my master. I then firmly believed that slavery was right and honorable. I now see very clearly the false position we were all in, both masters and slaves; and I look back, with utter astonishment, at the absurdity of the claims so arrogantly set up by the masters, over beings designed by God to be as free as kings; and at the perfect stupidity of the slave, in admitting for one moment the validity of these claims.

In obedience to my mother's instructions, I had educated myself to such a sense of honesty, that, when I had become a mother, I would sometimes whip my child when he cried to me for bread, rather than give it a piece secretly, lest it should learn to take what was not its own! I now know, from personal observation, that the slaveholders of the South feel it to be a religious duty to teach their slaves to be honest, and never to take what is not their own! Oh consistency, art thou not a jewel? Yet I gloried in the fact that I was faithful and true to my master. 'It made me true to my God'–meaning, that it helped to form in me a character that loved truth, and hated a lie, and had saved me from the bitter pains and fears that are sure to follow in the wake of insincerity and hypocrisy.

As I advanced in years, an attachment sprung up between me and a slave named Robert. But his master, an Englishman by the name of Catlin, anxious that no one's property but his own should be enhanced by the increase of his slaves, forbade Robert's visits, and commanded him to take a wife among his fellow servants. Notwithstanding this interdiction, Robert, following the bent of his inclinations, continued his visits to me, though very stealthily, and, as he believed, without exciting the suspicion of his master. But one Saturday afternoon, hearing that I was ill, he took the liberty to go and see me. The first intimation I had of his visit was the appearance of my master, inquiring 'if I had seen Bob.' When I answered in the negative, he said to me, 'If you see him, tell him to take care of himself, for the Catlins are after him.'

Almost at that instant, Bob made his appearance; and the first people he met were his old and his young masters. They were terribly enraged at finding him there, and the eldest began cursing, and calling upon his son to 'Knock down the d–d black rascal'; at the same time, they both fell upon him like tigers, beating him with the heavy ends of their canes, bruising and mangling his head and face in the most awful manner, and causing the blood, which streamed from his wounds, to cover him like a slaughtered beast, constituting him a most shocking spectacle. Mr. Dumont interposed at this point, telling the ruffians they could no longer thus spill human blood on his premises–he would have 'no niggers killed there.' The Catlins then took a rope they had taken with them for the purpose, and tied Bob's hands behind him in such a manner, that Mr. Dumont insisted on loosening the cord, declaring that no brute should be tied in that manner, where he was. And as they led him away, like the greatest of criminals, the more humane Dumont followed them to their homes, as Robert's protector; and when he returned, he kindly came to me to tell me he did not think they would strike him anymore, as their wrath had greatly cooled before he left them.

I had witnessed this scene from my window, and was greatly shocked at the murderous treatment of poor Robert, whom I truly loved, and whose only crime, in the eye of his persecutors, was his affection for me. This beating, and I know not what after treatment, completely subdued the spirit of its victim, for Robert ventured no more to visit me, but like an obedient and faithful chattel, took himself a wife from the house of his master. Robert did not live many years after his last visit, and took his departure to that "country", where 'they neither marry nor are given in marriage,' and where the oppressor cannot molest.

My marriage

Subsequently, I was married to a fellow-slave, named Thomas, who had previously had two wives, one of whom, if not both, had been torn from him and sold far away. And it is more than probable that he was not only allowed but encouraged to take another wife after each successive sale. Such was the custom among slaveholders at that time; and that in a twenty months' residence among them, we never knew anyone to open the lip against the practice; and when we severely censured it, the slaveholder had nothing to say; and the slave pleaded that, under existing circumstances, he could do no better.

As I have said, I was married to Thomas– I was, after the fashion of slavery, one of the slaves performing the ceremony for us; as no true minister of Christ can perform, as in the presence of God, what he knows to be a mere farce, a mock marriage, unrecognized by any civil law, and liable to be annulled any moment, when the interest or caprice of the master should dictate.

With what feelings must slaveholders expect us to listen to their horror of amalgamation in prospect, while they are well aware that we know how calmly and quietly they contemplate the present state of licentiousness their own wicked laws have created, not only as it regards the slave, but as it regards the more privileged portion of the population of the South?

Slaveholders appear to me to take the same notice of the vices of the slave, as one does of the vicious disposition of his horse. They are often an inconvenience; further than that, they care not to trouble themselves about the matter.

(Editor's Note: When there is no respect for the sanctity of the union between a man and a woman, and there is no respect for the institution of marriage and therefore, the family, neither between blacks or even between whites, when the white master thinks his right to bed his women slaves, regardless if he has a wife, the relations between people then becomes an irrational act, such as animals perform their coupling.)

I became a mother

In process of time, I found myself the mother of five children, and I rejoiced in being permitted to be the instrument of increasing the property of my oppressors! I can now declare of the slaves in their ignorance, that 'their thoughts are no longer than my finger.'

Think, dear reader, without a blush, if you can, for one moment, of a mother thus willingly, and with pride, laying her own children, the 'flesh of her flesh,' on the altar of slavery! But we must remember that beings capable of such sacrifices are not mothers on the eyes of their masters; they are only 'things,' 'chattels,' 'property.'

But since that time, I have made some advances from a state of chattelism towards that of a woman and a mother; and I now look back upon my thoughts and feelings there, in my state of ignorance and degradation, as one does on the dark imagery of a fitful dream. One moment it seems but a frightful illusion; again it appears a terrible reality. I wish to God it was but a dreamy myth, and not, as it now stands, a horrid reality to some three millions of chattelized human beings.

I have already alluded to my care not to teach my children to steal, by my example; and I say, with groanings that cannot be written, 'The Lord only knows how many times I let my children go hungry, rather than take secretly the bread I liked not to ask for.'

To me, my master's kindness of heart was absolute. If my master came into the house and found my infant crying, (as I could not always attend to its wants and the commands of my mistress at the same time,) he would turn to his wife with a look of reproof, and ask her why she did not see the child taken care of; saying, most earnestly, 'I will not hear this crying; I can't bear it, and I will not hear any child cry so. Here, Bell, (as he called me) take care of this child, if no more work is done for a week.' And he would linger to see if his orders were obeyed, and not countermanded.

When I went to the field to work, I used to put my infant in a basket, tying a rope to each handle, and suspending the basket to a branch of a tree, and set another small child to swing it. It was thus secure from reptiles and was easily administered to, and even lulled to sleep, by a child too young for other labors. Some white women were even quite struck with the ingenuity of such a baby-tender–apparently so much easier than the one they have in their more civilized homes; easier for the child, because it gets the motion without the least jar; and easier for the nurse, because the hammock is strung so high as to supersede the necessity of stooping.

Slaveholder's promises

After emancipation had been decreed by the State of New York, some years before the time fixed for its consummation, my master told me if I would do well, and be faithful, he would give me 'free papers,' one year before she was legally free by statute. In the year 1826, I had a badly diseased hand, which greatly diminished my usefulness; but on the arrival of July 4, 1827, the time specified for the receiving of my 'free papers,' I claimed the fulfillment of my master's promise; but he refused granting it, on account (as he alleged) of the loss he had sustained by my hand. I pleaded that I had worked all the time, and done many things I was not wholly able to do, although I knew I had been less useful than formerly; but my master remained inflexible. My very faithfulness probably operated against me now, and he found it less easy than he thought to give up the profits of his faithful Bell, who had so long done him efficient service.

But I inwardly determined that I would remain quietly with him only until I had spun his wool–about one hundred pounds–and then I would leave him, taking the rest of the time to myself. Ah! the slaveholders are TERRIBLE for promising to give you this or that, or such and such a privilege, if you will do thus and so; and when the time of fulfillment comes, and one claims the promise, they, indeed, recollect nothing of the kind: and you are, like as not, taunted with being a LIAR; or, at best, the slave is accused of not having performed his part or condition of the contract.

Oh! I have felt as if I could not live through the operation sometimes. Just think of us! so eager for our pleasures, and just foolish enough to keep feeding and feeding ourselves up with the idea that we should get what had been thus fairly promised; and when we think it is almost in our hands, find ourselves flatly denied! Just think! how could we bear it? Why, there was Charles Brodhead promised his slave Ned, that when harvesting was over, he might go and see his wife, who lived some twenty or thirty miles off. So Ned worked early and late, and as soon as the harvest was all in, he claimed the promised boon. His master said, he had merely told him he 'would see if he could go, when the harvest was over; but now he saw that he could not go.' But Ned, who still claimed a positive promise, on which he had fully depended, went on cleaning his shoes. His master asked him if he intended going, and on his replying 'yes,' took up a sled-stick that lay near him, and gave him such a blow on the head as broke his skull, killing him dead on the spot.

The poor colored people all felt struck down by the blow. Ah! and well they might. Yet it was but one of a long series of bloody, and other most effectual blows, struck against their liberty and their lives. No official notice was taken of his more than brutal murder. But to return from my digression.

I, therefore, was to have been free July 4, 1827, but I continued with my master till the wool was spun, and the heaviest of my freedom into my own hands, and seek my fortune in some other place.

My escape

The question in my mind, and one not easily solved, now was, 'How can I get away?' So, as was my usual custom, I 'told God I was afraid to go in the night, and in the day everybody would see me.' At length, the thought came to me that I could leave just before the day dawned, and get out of the neighborhood where I was known before the people were much astir. 'Yes,' I said to God fervently, 'that's a good thought! Thank you, God, for that thought!' So, receiving it as coming direct from God, I acted upon it, and one fine morning, a little before daybreak, I stepped stealthily away from the rear of Master Dumont's house, my infant on one arm and my wardrobe on the other; the bulk and weight of which, probably, I never found so convenient as on the present occasion, a cotton handkerchief containing both my clothes and my provisions.

As I gained the summit of a high hill, a considerable distance from my master's, the sun offended me by coming forth in all his pristine splendor. I thought it never was so light before; indeed, I thought it much too light. I stopped to look about me, and ascertain if my pursuers were yet in sight. No one appeared, and, for the first time, the question came up for settlement, 'Where, and to whom, shall I go?' In all my thoughts of getting away, I had not once asked myself whether I should direct my steps. I sat down, fed my infant, and again turning my thoughts to God, my only help, I prayed him to direct me to some safe asylum. And soon it occurred to me, that there was a man living somewhere in the direction I had been pursuing, by the name of Levi Rowe, whom I had known, and who, I thought, would be likely to befriend me.

I accordingly pursued my way to his house, where I found him ready to entertain and assist me, though he was then on his death-bed. He bade me to partake of the hospitalities of his house, said he knew of two good places where I might get in, and requested his wife to show me where they were to be found. As soon as I came in sight of the first house, I recollected having seen it and its inhabitants before, and instantly exclaimed, 'That's the place for me; I shall stop there.' I went there, and found the good people of the house, Mr. and Mrs. Van Wagener, absent, but was kindly received and hospitably entertained by their excellent mother, till the return of her children. When they arrived, she made my case known to them. They listened to my story, assuring me they never turned the needy away, and willingly gave me employment.

I had not been there long before my old master, Dumont, appeared, as I had anticipated; for when I took my leave of him, I resolved not to go too far from him, and not put him to as much trouble in looking her up–for the latter he was sure to do–as Tom and Jack had done when they ran away from him, a short time before. This was very considerate of me to say the least, and a proof that 'like begets like.' He had often considered my feelings, though not always, and I was equally considerate.

When my master saw me, he said, 'Well, Bell, so you've run away from me.' 'No, I did not run away; I walked away by daylight, and all because you had promised me a year of my time.' His reply was, 'You must go back with me.' MY decisive answer was,

'No, I won't go back with you.' He said, 'Well, I shall take the child.' This also was as stoutly negatived.

Mr. Isaac S. Van Wagener then interposed, saying, he had never been in the practice of buying and selling slaves; he did not believe in slavery; but, rather than have me taken back by force, he would buy her services for the balance of the year–for which my master charged twenty dollars, and five in addition for the child. The sum was paid, and my master Dumont departed; but not till he had heard Mr. Van Wagener tell me not to call him master–adding, 'there is but one master; and he who is your master is my master.'

I inquired what I should call him? He answered, 'call me Isaac Van Wagener, and my wife is Maria Van Wagener.' I could not understand this, and thought it a mighty change, as it most truly was from a master whose word was law, to simple Isaac S. Van Wagener, who was master to no one. With these noble people, who, though they could not be the masters of slaves, were undoubtedly a portion of God's nobility, I resided one year, and from them I derived the name of Van Wagener; he being my last master in the eye of the law, and a slave's surname is ever the same as his master; that is, if he is allowed to have any other name than Tom, Jack, or Guffin.

Slaves have sometimes been severely punished for adding their master's name to their own. But when they have no particular title to it, it is no particular offense.

Illegal sale of my son

A little previous to when I left my old master, he had sold my child, a boy of five years, to a Dr. Gedney, who took him with him as far as New York City, on his way to England; but finding the boy too small for his service, he sent him back to his brother, Solomon Gedney. This man disposed of him to his sister's husband, a wealthy planter, by the name of Fowler, who took him to his own home in Alabama.

This illegal and fraudulent transaction had been perpetrated some months before I knew of it, as I was now living at Mr. Van Wagener's. The law expressly prohibited the sale of any slave out of the

State,–and all minors were to be free at twenty-one years of age; and Mr. Dumont had sold Peter with the express understanding, that he was soon to return to the State of New York, and be emancipated at the specified time.

When I heard that my son had been sold to the South, I immediately started on foot and alone, to find the man who had thus dared, in the face of all law, human and divine, to sell my child out of the State; and if possible, to bring him to account for the deed.

Arriving at New Paltz, I went directly to my former mistress, Dumont, complaining bitterly of the removal of my son. My mistress heard me through, and then replied–'Ugh! a fine fuss to make about a little nigger! Why, haven't you as many of 'em left as you can see to, and take care of? A pity 'tis, the niggers are not all in Guinea!! Making such a halloo-balloo about the neighborhood; and all for a paltry nigger!!!'

I heard her through, and after a moment's hesitation, answered, in tones of deep determination–'I'll have my child again.' 'Have your child again!' repeated my mistress–her tones big with contempt, and scorning the absurd idea of me getting him.

'How can you get him? And what have you to support him with, if you could? Have you any money?' 'No,' I answered, 'I have no money, but God has enough, or what's better! And I'll have my child again.' These words were pronounced in the most slow, solemn, and determined measure and manner. And in speaking of it, I said to myself, 'Oh my God! I know I'd have him again.' I was sure God would help me to get him. Why, I felt so tall within–I felt as if the power of a nation was with me!

I could never be able to transmit into paper the impressions that I have when moved by lofty or deep feeling. I am unable to transfer the look, the gesture, the tone of voice, in connection to my plead, the fit expressions used, the spirit-stirring animation that, at such a time, pervaded all I said.

After leaving my mistress, I called on Mrs. Gedney, mother of him who had sold my boy; who, after listening to my lamentations, my grief being mingled with indignation at the sale of my son, and my declaration that I would have him again–said, 'Dear me! What a disturbance to make about your child! What, is your child, better than my child? My child is gone out there, and yours is gone to live with her, to have enough of everything, and be treated like a gentleman!'

And here she laughed at my absurd fears, as she would represent them to be. 'Yes,' I said, 'your child has gone there, but she is married, and my boy has gone as a slave, and he is too little to go so far from his mother. Oh, I must have my child.' And here the continued laugh of Mrs. G. seemed to me, in this time of anguish and distress, almost demoniacal. And well it was for Mrs. Gedney, that, at that time, she could not even dream of the awful fate awaiting her own beloved daughter, at the hands of him whom she had chosen as worthy the wealth of her love and confidence, and in whose society her young heart had calculated on a happiness, purer and more elevated than was ever conferred by a kingly crown. But, alas! she was doomed to disappointment, as I shall relate later.

At this point, I earnestly begged of God that he would show to those about me that He was my helper; and He did; or, if He did not show them, he did me.

Darkness before dawn

This homely proverb was illustrated to me soon enough for, at the period at which I have arrived in my narrative, to me, the darkness seemed palpable, and the waters of affliction covered my soul; yet light was about to break in upon me.

Soon after the scenes related in the last chapter, which had harrowed up my very soul to agony, I met a man, (we would like to tell you who, dear reader, but it would be doing him no kindness, even at the present day, to do so,) who evidently sympathized with me, and counseled me to go to the Quakers, telling me they were already feeling very indignant at the fraudulent sale of my son, and assuring me that they would readily assist me, and direct me what to do. He pointed out to me two houses, where lived some of those people, who formerly, more than any other sect, perhaps, lived out the principles of the gospel of Christ. I wended my way to their dwellings, was listened to, unknown as I personally was to them, with patience, and soon gained their sympathies and active co-operation.

They gave me lodgings for the night; and I must tell you how in awe I was of the nice, high, clean, white, beautiful bed they assigned me to sleep in, which contrasted so strangely with my former pallets, that I sat down and contemplated it, perfectly absorbed in wonder that such a bed should have been appropriated to one like myself. For some time I thought that I would lie down beneath it, on my usual bedstead, the floor. I did, indeed, and now I laugh heartily at my former self. However, I finally concluded to make use of the bed, for fear that not to do so might injure the feelings of my good hostess. In the morning, the Quaker saw that I was taken and set down near Kingston, with directions to go to the Court House, and enter a complaint to the Grand Jury.

By a little inquiry, I found which was the building I sought, went into the door, and taking to the first man I saw of imposing appearance for the grand jury, I commenced my complaint. But he very civilly informed me there was no Grand Jury there; I must go upstairs. When I had with some difficulty ascended the flight through the crowd that filled them, I again turned to the 'grandest' looking man I could select, telling him I had come to enter a complaint to the Grand Jury. For his own amusement, he inquired what my complaint was; but, when he saw it was a serious matter, he said to me, 'This is no place to enter a complaint–go in there,' pointing in a particular direction.

I then went in, where I found the Grand Jurors indeed sitting, and again commenced to relate my injuries. After holding some conversation among themselves, one of them rose, and bidding me to follow him, led the way to a side office, where he heard my story, and asked me 'if I could swear that the child I spoke of was my son?' 'Yes,' I answered, 'I swear it's my son.' 'Stop, stop!' said the lawyer, 'you must swear by this book'–giving me a book, which I think must have been the Bible. I took it, and putting it to my lips, began again to swear it was my child. The clerks, unable to preserve their gravity any longer, burst into an uproarious laugh; and one of them inquired of lawyer Chip of what use it could be to make me swear. 'It will answer the law,' replied the officer. He then made me comprehend just what he wished me to do, to put my hand over the book and then I took a lawful oath, as far as the outward ceremony could make it one. All can judge how far I understood its spirit and meaning.

He now gave me a writ, directing me to take it to the constable at New Paltz, and have him serve it on Solomon Gedney. I obeyed, walking, or rather trotting, in my haste, some eight or nine miles.

But while the constable, through mistake, served the writ on a brother of the real culprit, Solomon Gedney slipped into a boat, and was nearly across the North River, on whose banks we were standing, before the dull Dutch constable was aware of his mistake. Solomon Gedney, meanwhile, consulted a lawyer, who advised him to go to Alabama and bring back the boy, otherwise, it might cost him fourteen years' imprisonment, and a thousand dollars in cash. By this time, it is hoped he began to feel that selling slaves unlawfully was not so good a business as he had wished to find it. He secreted himself till due preparations could be made, and soon set sail for Alabama. Steamboats and railroads had not then annihilated distance to the extent they now have, and although he left in the fall of the year, spring came before he returned, bringing the boy with him—but holding on to him as his property.

It had ever been my prayer, not only that my son might be returned, but that he should be delivered from bondage, and into my own hands, lest he should be punished out of mere spite to me, who was so greatly annoying and irritating to my oppressors; and if my suit was gained, my very triumph would add vastly to their irritation.

Therefore, I again sought advice of Esquire Chip, whose counsel was, that the aforesaid constable serves the before-mentioned writ upon the right person. This being done, soon brought Solomon Gedney up to Kingston, where he gave bonds for his appearance at court, in the sum of $600.

Esquire Chip next informed me, that my case must now lie over till the next session of the court, some months in the future. 'The law must take its course,' said he.
'What! wait another court! wait months?' I said persevering. 'Why, long before that time, he can go clear off, and take my child with him—no one knows where. I cannot wait; I must have him now, whilst he is to be had.'
'Well,' said the lawyer, very coolly, 'if he puts the boy out of the way, he must pay the $600—one half of which will be yours'; supposing, perhaps, that $300 would pay for a 'heap of children,' in the eye of

a slave who never, in all her life, called a dollar her own.

But in this instance, he was mistaken in his reckoning. I assured him, that I had not been seeking money, neither would money satisfy me; it was my son, and my son alone I wanted, and my son I must have. Neither could I wait court, not I.

The lawyer used his every argument to convince me, that I ought to be very thankful for what they had done for me; that it was a great deal, and it was but reasonable that I should now wait patiently the time of the court. Yet I never felt, for a moment, like being influenced by these suggestions. I felt my prayer, the burden of which had been–'O Lord, give my son into my hands, and that speedily! Let not the spoilers have him any longer.'

Notwithstanding, I very distinctly saw that those who had thus far helped me on so kindly were wearied of me, and I feared God was wearied also. I had a short time previous learned that Jesus was a Saviour, and an intercessor; and I thought that if Jesus could but be induced to plead for me in the present trial.

As I was walking about, scarcely knowing whither I went, asking within myself, 'Who will show me any good, and lend a helping hand in this matter,' I was accosted by a perfect stranger, and one whose name I have never learned, in the following terms: 'Halloo, there; how do you get along with your boy? do they give him up to you?'

I told him all, adding that now everybody was tired, and I had none to help me. He said, 'Look here! I'll tell you what you'd better do. Do you see that stone house yonder?' pointing in a particular direction. 'Well, lawyer Demain lives there, and do you go to him, and lay your case before him; I think he'll help you. Stick to him. Don't give him peace till he does. I feel sure if you press him, he'll do it for you.'

I needed no further urging, but trotted off at my peculiar gait in the direction of his house, as fast as possible,–for I was not encumbered with stockings, shoes, or any other heavy article of dress. When I had told him my story, in my impassioned manner, he looked at me a few moments, as if to ascertain if he were contemplating a new variety of humans, and then told me, if I would give him five dollars, he would get my son for me, in twenty-four hours.

'Why,' I replied, 'I have no money, and never had a dollar in my life!'

Said he, 'If you will go to those Quakers in Poppletown, who carried you to court, they will help you to five dollars in cash, I have no doubt; and you shall have your son in twenty-four hours, from the time you bring me that sum.'

I completed the journey to Poppletown, a distance of some ten miles, very expeditiously; collected considerable more than the sum specified by the barrister; then, shutting the money tightly in my hand, I trotted back, and paid the lawyer a larger fee than he had demanded. When inquired of by people what I had done with the overplus, I answered, 'Oh, I got it for lawyer Demain, and I gave it to him. ' They assured me I was a fool to do so; that I should have kept all over five dollars, and purchased myself shoes with it. 'Oh, I do not want money or clothes now, I only want my son; and if five dollars will get him, more will surely get him. ' And if the lawyer had returned it to me, I swear I would not have accepted it. I was perfectly willing he should have every coin I could raise, if he would but restore my lost son to me. Moreover, the five dollars he required were for the remuneration of him who should go after my son and his master, and not for his own services.

The lawyer now renewed his promise, that I should have my son in twenty-four hours. But I, having no idea of this space of time, went several times in a day, to ascertain if my son had come. Once, when the servant opened the door and saw me, she said, in a tone expressive of much surprise, 'Why, this woman's come again!' I then wondered if I went too often. When the lawyer appeared, he told me the twenty-four hours would not expire till the next morning; if I would call then, I would see my son.

The next morning saw me at the lawyer's door, while he was yet in his bed. He now assured me it was morning till noon; and that before noon my son would be there, for he had sent the famous 'Matty Styles' after him, who would not fail to have the boy and his master on hand in due season, either dead or alive; of that he was sure. Telling me I need not come again; he would himself inform me of their arrival.

After dinner, he appeared at Mr. Rutzer's, (a place the lawyer had procured for me, while I awaited the arrival of my boy,) assuring me that my son had come; but that he stoutly denied having any mother, or any relatives in that place; and said, 'she must go over and identify him.'

She went to the office, but at sight of her, the boy cried aloud, and regarded her as some terrible being, who was about to take him away from a kind and loving friend. He knelt, even, and begged them, with tears, not to take him away from his dear master, who had brought him from the dreadful South, and been so kind to him.

When he was questioned relative to the bad scar on his forehead, he said, 'Fowler's horse hove him.' And of the one on his cheek, 'That was done by running against the carriage.' In answering these questions, he looked imploringly at his master, as much as to say, 'If they are falsehoods, you bade me say them; may they be satisfactory to you, at least.'

The justice, noting his appearance, bade him forget his master and attend only to him. But the boy persisted in denying his mother, and clinging to his master, saying his mother did not live in such a place as that.

However, they allowed me to identify him, my son; and Esquire Demain pleaded that he claimed the boy for me, on the ground that he had been sold out of the State, contrary to the laws in such cases made and provided–spoke of the penalties annexed to said crime, and of the sum of money the delinquent was to pay, in case anyone chose to prosecute him for the offense he had committed.

I was sitting in a corner, scarcely daring to breathe, thought within myself, 'If I can but get the boy, the $200 may remain for whoever else chooses to prosecute–I have done enough to make myself enemies already'–and I trembled at the thought of the formidable enemies I had probably arrayed against myself–helpless and despised as I was.

When the pleading was at an end, I understood the Judge to declare, as the sentence of the Court, that the 'boy be delivered into the hands of the mother–having no other master, no other controller, no other conductor, but his mother.' This sentence was obeyed; he was delivered into my hands, the boy meanwhile begging, most piteously, not to be taken from his dear master, saying I was not his mother, and that his mother did not live in such a place as that. And it was some time before lawyer Demain, the clerks, and I, could collectively succeed in calming the child's fears, and in convincing him that I was not some terrible monster, as he had for the last months, probably, been trained to believe; and who, in taking him away from his master, was taking him from all good, and consigning him to all evil.

When at last kind words and bon-bons had quieted his fears, and he could listen to their explanations, he said to me– 'Well, you do look like my mother used to'; and I was soon able to make him comprehend some of the obligations he was under, and the relation he stood in, both to myself and his master. I commenced as soon as practicable to examine the boy, and found, to my utter astonishment, that from the crown of his head to the sole of his foot, the callosities and indurations on his entire body were most frightful to behold. His back was like her fingers, as she laid them side by side.

'Heavens! what is all this?' I said. He answered, 'It is where Fowler whipped, kicked, and beat me.' She exclaimed, 'Oh, Lord Jesus, look! see my poor child! Oh Lord, "render unto them double" for all this! Oh my God! Pete, how did you bear it?'

'Oh, this is nothing, mammy–if you should see Phillis, I guess you'd scare! She had a little baby, and Fowler cut her till the milk as well as blood ran down her body. You would scare to see Phillis, mammy.'

When I inquired, 'What did Miss Eliza Fowler say, Pete, when you were treated so badly?' he replied, 'Oh, mammy, she said she wished I was with Bell. Sometimes I crawled under the stoop, mammy, the blood running all about me, and my back would stick to the boards; and sometimes Miss Eliza would come and grease my sores, when all were in bed and asleep.'

Death of Mrs. Eliza Fowler

As soon as possible I procured a place for Peter, as tender of locks, at a place called Wahkendall, near Greenkills. After he was thus disposed of, I visited my sister Sophia, who resided at Newberg, and spent the winter with several different families with whom I was acquainted. I remained some time in the family of Mr. Latin, who was a relative of Solomon Gedney; and the latter, when he found out that I was staying with his cousin, used all his influence to persuade him that I was a great mischief-maker and a very troublesome person,–that I had put him to some hundreds of dollars expense, by fabricating lies about him, and especially his sister and her family, concerning my boy, when the latter was living so like a gentleman with them; and, for his part, he would not advise his friends to harbor or encourage me. However, his cousins, the Latins, could not see with the eyes of his feelings, and consequently his words fell powerless on them, and they retained me in their service as long as they had aught for me to do.

I then went to visit my former master, Dumont. I had scarcely arrived there, when Mr. Fred Waring entered, and seeing me, pleasantly accosted me, and asked 'what I was driving at now-a-days.' When I answered 'nothing particular,' he requested me to go over to his place, and assist his folks, as some of them were sick, and they needed an extra hand. I very gladly assented. When Mr. Waring retired, my master wanted to know why I wished to help people, that called me the 'worst of devils,' as Mr. Waring had done in the courthouse–for he was the uncle of Solomon Gedney, and attended the trial I have described.

He declared that I was a fool to; he wouldn't do it. 'Oh,' I told him, 'I would not mind that, since I was very glad to have people forget their anger toward me.'

I went over, but too happy to feel that their ressentiment was passed, and commenced my work with a light heart and a strong will. I had not worked long in this frame of mind, before a young daughter of Mr. Waring rushed into the rooms exclaiming, with uplifted hands–'Heavens and earth, Isabella! Fowler's murdered Cousin Eliza!' 'Ho,' I said, 'that's nothing–he liked to have killed my child; nothing saved him but God.'

What I meant was that I was not at all surprised at it, for a man whose heart was sufficiently hardened to treat a mere child as mine had been treated, was, in my opinion, more evil than human, and prepared for the commission of any crime that his passions might prompt him to.

The child further informed me that a letter had arrived by mail bringing the news.

Immediately after this announcement, Solomon Gedney and his mother came in, going direct to Mrs. Waring's room, where I soon heard tones as of someone reading. Something said to me inwardly, 'Go upstairs and hear.' At first, I hesitated, but it seemed to press me the more–'Go up and hear!' I went up, unusual as it is for slaves to leave their work and enter unbidden their mistress's room, for the sole purpose of seeing or hearing what may be seen or heard there. But on this occasion, I walked in at the door, shut it, placed my back against it, and listened. I saw them and heard them read–'He knocked her down with his fist, jumped on her with his knees, broke her collar-bone, and tore out her wind-pipe! He then attempted his escape, but was pursued and arrested, and put in an iron bank for safe-keeping!' And the friends were requested to go down and take away the poor innocent children who had thus been made in one short day more than orphans.

When I had heard the letter, all being too much absorbed in their own feelings to take note of me, I returned to my work, my heart swelling with conflicting emotions. I was awed at the dreadful deed; I mourned the fate of the loved Eliza, who had in such an undeserved and barbarous manner been put away from her labors and watchings as a tender mother; and, 'last though not least,' in the development of my character and spirit, my heart bled for the afflicted relatives; especially her mother, even though we 'laughed at my calamity, and mocked me when my fear came.'

My thoughts dwelt long and intently on the subject, and the wonderful chain of events that had conspired to bring me that day to that house, to listen to that piece of intelligence–to that house, where I never was before or afterwards in my life, and invited there by people who had so lately been hotly incensed against me. It all seemed very remarkable to me, and I viewed it as flowing from a special providence of God. I thought I saw clearly, that their unnatural bereavement was a blow dealt in retributive justice; but I found it not in my heart to exult or rejoice over it. I felt as if God had more than answered my petition, when I asked, in my anguish of mind, 'Oh, Lord, render unto them double!' I dared not find fault with God, exactly; but the language of my heart was, 'Oh, my God! that's too much–I did not mean quite so much, God!' It was a terrible blow to the friends of the deceased; and her selfish mother went deranged, and walking to and fro in her delirium, called aloud for her poor murdered daughter–'Eliza! Eliza!'

The derangement of Mrs. G. was not matter of hearsay, as I saw her after the trial; and I has no reason to doubt the truth of what I heard. I could never learn the subsequent fate of Fowler, but heard, in the spring of '49, that his children had been seen in Kingston–one of whom was spoken of as a fine, interesting girl, albeit a halo of sadness fell like a veil about her.

My religious experience

I will now turn from the outward and temporal to my inward and spiritual life. It is ever both interesting and instructive to trace the exercises of a human mind, through the trials and mysteries of life.

My mother, as I have already said, talked to me of God. From these conversations, my incipient mind drew the conclusion, that God was 'a great man'; greatly superior to other men in power; and being located 'high in the sky,' could see all that transpired on the earth. I believed he not only saw, but noted down all my actions in a great book, even as my master kept a record of whatever he wished not to forget. But I had no idea that God knew my thoughts till I had uttered them aloud.

As I have before mentioned, I had ever been mindful of my mother's injunctions, spreading out in detail all my troubles before God, imploring and firmly trusting him to send my deliverance from them. While yet a child, I listened to a story of a wounded soldier, left alone in the trail of a flying army, helpless and starving, who hardened the very ground about him with kneeling in his supplications to God for relief, until it arrived. From this story, I was deeply impressed with the idea, that if I also were to present my petitions under the open canopy of heaven, speaking very loud, I should the more readily be heard; consequently, I sought a fitting spot for this, my rural sanctuary. The place I selected, in which to offer up my daily prayers, was a small island in a small stream, covered with large willow shrubbery, beneath which the sheep had made their pleasant winding paths; and sheltering themselves from the scorching rays of a noontide sun, luxuriated in the cool shadows of the graceful willows, as they listened to the tiny falls of the silver waters.

It was a lonely spot, and chosen for its beauty, its retirement, and because I thought that there, in the noise of those waters, I could speak louder to God, without being overheard by any who might pass that way. When I had made choice of my sanctum, at a point of the island where the stream met, after having been separated, I improved it by pulling away the branches of the shrubs from the centre, and weaving them together for a wall on the outside, forming a circular arched alcove, made entirely of the graceful willow. To this place I resorted daily, and in pressing times much more frequently.

At this time, my prayers, or, more appropriately, 'talks with God,' were perfectly original and unique, and would be well worth preserving, were it possible to give the tones and manner with the words; but no adequate idea of them can be written while the tones and manner remain inexpressible.

I would sometimes repeat, 'Our Father in heaven,' in my Low Dutch, as taught to me by my mother; after that, all was from the suggestions of my own rude mind. I related to God, in minute detail, all my troubles and sufferings, inquiring, as I proceeded, 'Do you think that's right, God?' and closed by begging to be delivered from the evil, whatever it might be.

I talked to God as familiarly as if he had been a creature like myself; and a thousand times more so, than if I had been in the presence of some earthly ruler. I demanded, with little expenditure of reverence or fear, a supply of all my more pressing wants, and at times my demands approached very near to commands. I felt as if God was under obligation to me, much more than I was to him. He seemed to my benighted vision in some manner bound to do my bidding.

My heart recoils now, with very dread, when I recall those shocking conversations with God. But to me, they were glorious, because my mind combined his infinite character of the tender father with the omniscient and omnipotent Creator of the universe.

I at first commenced promising God, that if he would help me out of all my difficulties, I would pay him by being very good; and this goodness I intended as a remuneration to God, and this I soon found much more easily promised than performed.

Days wore away–new trials came–God's aid was invoked, and the same promises repeated; and every successive night found my part of the contract unfulfilled. I now began to excuse myself, by telling God I could not be good in my present circumstances; but if he would give me a new place, and a good master and mistress, I could and would be good; and I expressly stipulated, that I would be good one day to show God how good I would be all of the time, when he should surround me with the right influences, and I should be delivered from the temptations that then so sorely beset me. But, alas! when night came, and I became conscious that I had yielded to all her temptations, and entirely failed of keeping my word with God, having prayed and promised one hour, and fallen into the sins of anger and profanity the next, the mortifying reflection weighed on my mind, and blunted my enjoyment. Still, I did not lay it deeply to heart, but continued to repeat my demands for aid, and my promises of pay, with full purpose of heart, at each particular time, that that day I would not fail to keep my plighted word.

Thus perished the inward spark, like a flame just igniting, when one waits to see whether it will burn on or die out, till the long desired change came, and I found myself in a new place, with a good mistress, and one who never instigated an otherwise kind master to be unkind to me; in short, a place where I had literally nothing to complain of, and where, for a time, I was more happy than I could well express. Oh, everything there was so pleasant, and kind, and good, and all so comfortable; enough of everything; indeed, it was beautiful!'

Here, at Mr. Van Wagener's,–as the reader will readily perceive I must have been,–I was so happy and satisfied, that God was entirely forgotten. Why should my thoughts turn to him, who was only known to me as a help in trouble? I had no trouble now; my every prayer had been answered in every minute particular. I had been delivered from my persecutors and temptations, my youngest child had been given to me, and the others I knew I had no means of sustaining if I had them with me, and was content to leave them were they were. Their father, who was much older than me, and who preferred serving his time out in slavery, to the trouble and dangers of the course I pursued, remained with the children and could keep an eye on them–though it is comparatively little that they can do for each other while they remain in slavery; and this little the slave, like persons in every other situation of life, is not always disposed to perform.

There are slaves, who, copying the selfishness of their superiors in power, in their conduct towards their fellows who may be thrown upon their mercy, by infirmity or illness, allow them to suffer for want of that kindness and care which it is fully in their power to render them.

The slaves in this country have ever been allowed to celebrate the principal, if not some of the lesser festivals observed by the Catholics and Church of

England;–many of them not being required to do the least service for several days, and at Christmas they have almost universally an entire week to themselves, except, perhaps, the attending to a few duties, which are absolutely required for the comfort of the families they belong to. If much service is desired, they are hired to do it, and paid for it as if they were free. The more sober portion of them spend these holidays in earning a little money. Most of them visit and attend parties and balls, and not a few of them spend it in the lowest dissipation. This respite from toil is granted them by all religionists, of whatever persuasion, and probably originated from the fact that many of the first slaveholders were members of the Church of England.

Frederick Douglass, who has devoted his great heart and noble talents entirely to the furtherance of the cause of his down-trodden race, has said–'From what I know of the effect of their holidays upon the slave, I believe them to be among the most effective means, in the hands of the slaveholder, in keeping down the spirit of insurrection. Were the slaveholders at once to abandon this practice, I have not the slightest doubt it would lead to an immediate insurrection among the slaves. These holidays serve as conductors, or safety-valves, to carry off the rebellious spirit of enslaved humanity. But for these, the slave would be forced up to the wildest desperation; and woe betide the slaveholder, the day he ventures to remove or hinder the operation of those conductors! I warn him that, in such an event, a spirit will go forth in their midst, more to be dreaded than the most appalling earthquake.'

When I had been at Mr. Van Wagener's a few months, I saw in prospect one of the festivals approaching. I know it by none but the Dutch name, Pingster–but I think it must have been Whitsuntide, in English.

I looked back to the time we celebrated those festivals back when I lived with master Dumont and everything looked so pleasant in my mind, as I saw retrospectively all my former companions enjoying their freedom for at least a little space, as well as their wonted convivialities, and in my heart I longed to be with them. With this picture before my mind's eye, I contrasted the quiet, peaceful life I was living with the excellent people of Wahkendall, and it seemed so dull and void of incident, that the very contrast served but to heighten my desire to return, that, at least, I might enjoy with them, once more, the coming festivities. These feelings had occupied a secret corner of my breast for some time, when, one morning, I told Mrs. Van Wagener that my old master Dumont would come that day, and that I should go home with him on his return. They expressed some surprise, and asked me where I had obtained my information. I replied that no one had told me, but I felt that he would come.

It seemed to have been one of those events that cast their shadows before; for, before night, Mr. Dumont made his appearance. I informed him of my intention to accompany him home. He answered, with a smile, 'I shall not take you back again; you ran away from me.' Thinking his manner contradicted his words, I did not feel repulsed, but made myself and child ready; and when my former master had seated himself in the open wagon, I walked towards it, intending to place myself and my child in the rear, and go with him. But, before I reached the vehicle, God revealed himself to me, with all the suddenness of a flash of lightning, showing me, in the twinkling of an eye, that he was all over–that he pervaded the universe–and that there was no place where God was not. I became instantly conscious of my great sin in forgetting my almighty Friend and ever-present help in time of trouble. All my unfulfilled promises arose before me, like a vexed sea whose waves run mountains high; and my soul, which seemed but one mass of lies, shrunk back aghast from the awful reproachable look of Him whom I had formerly talked to, as if he had been a being like myself.

A dire dread of annihilation now seized me and I waited to see if, by 'another look,' I was to be stricken from existence,–swallowed up, even as the fire licketh up the oil with which it comes in contact. When at last the second look came not, and my attention was once more called to outward things, I observed my master had left, and exclaiming aloud, 'Oh, God, I did not know you were so big,' I walked back into the house, and made an effort to resume my work.

Hard times

Now you see me, my youngest daughter, and my only son, in possession of, at least, our nominal freedom. But what can we do with it? We still depended on our masters for work and sustenance. It has been said that the freedom of the most free of the colored people of this country is but nominal; but stinted and limited as it is, at best, it is an immense remove from chattel slavery. This fact is disputed, I know; but I have no confidence in the honesty of such questionings.

My husband, quite advanced in age, and infirm of health, was emancipated, with the balance of the adult slaves of the State, according to law, the following summer, July 4, 1828. For a few years after this event, he was able to earn a scanty living, and when he failed to do that, he was dependent on the 'world's cold charity,' and died in a poorhouse.

I had myself and two children to provide for; my wages were trifling, for at that time the wages of females were at a small advance from nothing; and I doubtless had to learn the first elements of economy–for what slaves, that were never allowed to make any stipulations or calculations for themselves, ever possessed an adequate idea of the true value of time, or, in fact, of any material thing in the universe? To such, 'prudent using' is meanness, and 'saving' is a word to be sneered at.

Of course, it was not in my power to make a home for myself, around whose sacred hearth-stone I could collect my children, as they gradually emerged from their prison-house of bondage; a home, where I could cultivate their affection, administer to their wants, and instill into their opening minds those principles of virtue, and that love of purity, truth and benevolence, which must forever form the foundation of a life of usefulness and happiness.

No–all this was far beyond my power or means, in more senses than one; and it should be taken into the account, whenever a comparison is instituted between the progress made by my children in virtue and goodness, and the progress of those who have been nurtured in the genial warmth of a sunny home, where good influences cluster, and bad ones are carefully excluded–where self-denying parents can bring to bear on one of the dearest objects of a parent's life, the promotion of the welfare of their children.

But God forbid that this suggestion should be wrested from its original intent, and made to shield anyone from merited rebuke! My children are now of an age to know good from evil, and may easily inform themselves on any point where they may yet be in doubt; and if they now suffer themselves to be drawn by temptation into the paths of the destroyer, or forget what is due to the mother who has done and suffered so much for them, and who, now that she is descending into the vale of years, and feels her health and strength declining, will turn her expecting eyes to them for aid and comfort, just as instinctly as the child turns its confiding eye to its fond parent, when it seeks for succor or sympathy–(for it is now their turn to do the work, and bear the burdens of life, so all must bear them in turn, as the wheel of life rolls on)–if, I say, they forget this, their duty and their happiness, and pursue an opposite course of sin and folly, they must lose the respect of the wise and good, and find, when too late, that 'the way of the transgressor is hard.'

I hope the reader will pardon this passing homily. I will now return to my narrative.

New trials

I was saying that the daydreams me and my husband cherished–the plan we drew of what we would do, and the comforts we thought to have, when we should obtain our freedom, and a little home of our own–had all turned to 'thin air' by the postponement of our freedom to so late a day. These delusive hopes were never to be realized, and a new set of trials was gradually to open before me. These were the heart-wasting trials of watching over my children, scattered, and imminently exposed to the temptations of the adversary, with few, if any, fixed principles to sustain them.

Oh, how little did I know myself of the best way to instruct and counsel them! Yet I did the best I then knew, when with them. I took them to the religious meetings; I talked to, and prayed for and with them; when they did wrong, I scolded at and whipped them.

Me and my son had been free about a year, when we went to reside in the city of New York; a place which I would doubtless have avoided, could I have seen what was there in store for me; for this view into the future would have taught me what I only learned by bitter experience, that the baneful influences going up from such a city were not the best helps to education, commenced as the education of her children had been.

My son Peter was, at the time of which we are speaking, just at that age when no lad should be subjected to the temptations of such a place, unprotected as he was, save by the feeble arm of a mother, herself a servant there. He was growing up to be a tall, well-formed, active lad, of quick perceptions, mild and cheerful in his disposition, with much that was open, generous and winning about him, but with little power to withstand temptation, and a ready ingenuity to provide himself with ways and means to carry out his plans, and conceal from his mother and her friends, all such as he knew would not meet their approbation. As will be readily believed, he was soon drawn into a circle of associates who did not improve either his habits or his morals.

Two years passed before I knew what character Peter was establishing for himself among his low and worthless comrades–passing under the assumed name of Peter Williams; and I began to feel a parent's pride in the promising appearance of my only son. But, alas! this pride and pleasure were shortly dissipated, as distressing facts relative to him came one by one to my astonished ear.

A friend of mine, a lady, who was much pleased with the good humor, ingenuity, and open confessions of Peter, when driven into a corner, and who, she said, 'was so smart, he ought to have an education, if anyone ought,'–paid ten dollars, as tuition fee, for him to attend a navigation school.

But Peter, little inclined to spend his leisure hours in study, when he might be enjoying himself in the dance, or otherwise, with his boon companions, went regularly and made some plausible excuses to the teacher, who received them as genuine, along with the ten dollars of my lady friend –, and while my friend and I believed him improving at school, he was, to our latent sorrow, improving in a very different place or places, and on entirely opposite principles.

We also procured him an excellent place as a coachman. But, wanting money, he sold his livery, and other things belonging to his master; who, having conceived a kind regard for him, considered his youth, and prevented the law from falling, with all its rigor, upon his head. Still, he continued to abuse his privileges, and to involve himself in repeated difficulties, from which I as often extricated him. At each time, I talked much, and reasoned and remonstrated with him; and he would, with such perfect frankness, lay open his whole soul to me, telling me he had never intended doing harm,–how he had been led along, little by little, till, before he was aware, he found himself in trouble–how he had tried to be good–and how, when he would have been so, 'evil was present with him,'– indeed he knew not how it was.

I, beginning to feel that the city was no place for him, urged his going to sea, and would have shipped him on board a man-of-war; but Peter was not disposed to consent to that proposition, while the city and its pleasures were accessible to him. I now became a prey to distressing fears, dreading lest the next day or hour come fraught with the report of some dreadful crime, committed or abetted by my son.

I thank the Lord for sparing me that giant sorrow, as all his wrongdoings never ranked higher, in the eye of the law, than misdemeanors. But as I could see no improvement in Peter, as a last resort, I resolved to leave him, for a time, unassisted, to bear the penalty of his conduct, and see what effect that would have on him. In the trial hour, I remained firm in my resolution. Peter again fell into the hands of the police, and sent for his mother, as usual; but I did not went to his relief. In his extremity, he sent for Peter Williams, a respectable colored barber, whose name he had been wearing, and who sometimes helped young culprits out of their troubles, and sent them from city dangers, by shipping them on board of whaling vessels (a very lucrative business, since whale oil is used to light lamps).

The curiosity of this man was awakened by the culprit's bearing his own name. He went to the Tombs and inquired into his case, but could not believe what Peter told him respecting his mother and family. Yet he redeemed him, and Peter promised to leave New York in a vessel that was to sail in the course of a week. He came to see me, and informed me of what had happened to him. I listened incredulously, as to an idle tale. He asked me to go with him and see for myself. I went, giving no credence to his story till I found myself in the presence of Mr. Williams, and heard him saying to me, 'I am very glad I have assisted your son; he stood in great need of sympathy and assistance; but I could not think he had such a mother here, although he assured me he had.'

My great trouble now was, a fear lest my son should deceive his benefactor, and be missing when the vessel sailed; but he begged me earnestly to trust him, for he said he had resolved to do better, and meant to abide by the resolve. My heart gave me no peace till the time of sailing, when Peter sent Mr. Williams and another messenger whom I knew, to tell me he had sailed.

But for a month afterwards, I looked to see him emerging from some by-place in the city, and appearing before me; so afraid was I that he was still unfaithful, and doing wrong. But he did not appear, and at length, I believed him really gone. He left in the summer of 1839, and his friends heard nothing further from him till I received the following letter, dated 'October 17, 1840';–

'MY DEAR AND BELOVED MOTHER:
'I take this opportunity to write to you and inform you that I am well, and in hopes for to find you the same. I am got on board the same unlucky ship Done, of Nantucket. I am sorry for to say, that I have been punished once severely, by shoving my head in the fire for other folks. We have had bad luck, but in hopes to have better. We have about 230 on board, but in hopes, if don't have good luck, that my parents will receive me with thanks. I would like to know how my sisters are. Does my cousins live in New York yet? Have you got my letter? If not, in- quire to Mr. Pierce Whiting's. I wish you would write me an answer as soon as possible. I am your only son, that is so far from your home, in the wide briny ocean. I have seen more of the world than ever I expected, and if I ever should return home safe, I will tell you all my troubles and hardships. Mother, I hope you do not forget me, your dear and only son. I should like

to know how Sophia, and Betsey, and Hannah, come on. I hope you all will forgive me for all that I have done.
Your son,
PETER VAN WAGENER.'

Another letter reads as follows, dated 'March 22, 1841':–
'MY DEAR MOTHER:
'I take this opportunity to write to you, and inform you that I have been well and in good health. I have wrote you a letter before, but have received no answer from you, and was very anxious to see you. I hope to see you in a short time. I have had very hard luck, but are in hopes to have better in time to come. I should like if my sisters are well, and all the people round the neighborhood. I expect to be home in twenty-two months or thereabouts. I have seen Samuel Laterett. Beware! There has happened very bad news to tell you, that Peter Jackson is dead. He died within two days' sail of Otaheite, one of the Society Islands. The Peter Jackson that used to live at Laterett's; he died on board the ship Done, of Nantucket, Captain Miller, in the latitude 15 53, and longitude 148 30 W. I have no more to say at present, but write as soon as possible.
Your only son,
PETER VAN WAGENER.

Another, containing the last intelligence I have had from my son, reads as follows, and was dated 'Sept. 19, 1841':–

'DEAR MOTHER:
'I take the opportunity to write to you and inform you that I am well and in good health, and in hopes to find you in the same. This is the fifth letter that I have wrote to you, and have received no answer, and it makes me very uneasy. So pray write as quick as you can, and tell me how all the people is about the neighborhood. We are out from home twenty-three months, and in hope to be home in fifteen months. I have not much to say; but tell me if you have been up home since I left or not. I want to know what sort of a time is at home. We had very bad luck when we first came out, but since we have had very good; so I am in hopes to do well yet; but if I don't do well, you need not expect me home these five years. So write as quick as you can, won't you? So now I am going to put an end to my writing, at present. Notice–when this you see, remember me, and place me in your mind.

Get me to my home, that's in the far distant west,

To the scenes of my childhood, that I like the best;
There the tall cedars grow, and the bright waters flow,
Where my parents will greet me, white man, let me go!
Let me go to the spot where the cateract plays,
Where oft I have sported in my boyish days;
And there is my poor mother, whose heart ever flows,
At the sight of her poor child, to her let me go, let me go!
Your only son,
PETER VAN WAGENER.

Since the date of the last letter, I has heard no tidings from my long-absent son, though ardently does my mother's heart long for such tidings, as my thoughts follow him around the world, in his perilous vocation, saying within myself– 'He is good now, I have no doubt; I feel sure that he has persevered, and kept the resolve he made before he left home;– he seemed so different before he went, so determined to do better.' His letters are inserted here for preservation, in case they prove the last I ever hear from him in this world.

finding a brother and sister

When I obtained the freedom of my son from Salomon, I remained in Kingston, where I had been drawn by the judicial process, about a year, during which time I became a member of the Methodist Church there: and when I went to New York, I took a letter missive from that church to the Methodist Church in John Street. Afterwards, I withdrew my connection with that church, and joined Zion's Church in Church Street, composed entirely of colored people. With the latter church, I remained until I went to reside with Mr. Pierson.

While I was in New York, my sister Sophia came from Newberg to reside in the former place. I had been favored with occasional interviews with this sister, although at one time I lost sight of her for the space of seventeen years–almost the entire period of my staying at Mr. Dumont's–and when she appeared before me again, handsomely dressed, I did not recognize her, till informed who she was. Sophia informed me that our brother Michael–a brother I had never seen–was in the city; and when she introduced him to me, he informed me that another sister, Nancy, had been living in the city, and had deceased a few months before. He described her features, her dress, her manner, and said she had for some time been a member of Zion's Church, naming the class she belonged to. I almost instantly recognized her as a sister in the church, with whom I had knelt at the altar, and with whom I had exchanged the speaking pressure of the hand, in recognition of their spiritual sisterhood; little thinking, at the time, that we were also children of the same earthly parents– Bomefree and Mau-mau Bett.

As inquiries and answers rapidly passed, and the conviction deepened that this was our sister, the very sister we had heard so much of, but had never seen, (for she was the self-same sister that had been locked in the great old-fashioned sleigh-box, when she was taken away, never to behold her mother's face again this side of the spirit-land, and Michael, the narrator, was the brother who had shared her fate,) I thought, 'D–h! here she was; we met; and was I not, at the time, struck with the peculiar feeling of her hand–the bony hardness so just like mine? and yet I could not know she was my sister; and now I see she looked so like my mother.' And I wept, and not alone; Sophia wept, and the strong man, Michael, mingled his tears with ours.

'Oh Lord,' I inquired, 'what is this slavery, that it can do such dreadful things? what evil can it not do?' Well, may I ask, for surely the evils it can and does do, daily and hourly, can never be summed up, till we can see them as they are recorded by those who write about them with no errors, and reckons without mistake. This account, my story, which now varies so widely in the estimate of different minds, I hope will be viewed alike by all.

Perhaps the pioneers in the slave's cause will be as much surprised as any to find that with all their looking, there remained so much unseen.

Gleanings

There are some hard things that crossed my life while in slavery, that I have no desire to publish for various reasons. First, because the parties from whose hands I suffered them have rendered up their account to a higher tribunal, and their innocent friends alone are living, to have their feelings injured by the recital. Secondly, because they are not all for the public ear, from their very nature. Thirdly, and not least, because if I were to tell all that happened to me as a slave–all that I know is 'God's truth'–it would seem to others, especially the uninitiated, so unaccountable, so unreasonable, and what is usually called so unnatural, (though it may be questioned whether people do not always act naturally,) they would not easily believe it. Why, no! they'd call me a liar! they would, indeed! and I do not wish to say anything to destroy my own character for veracity, though what I say is strictly true.

Some things have been omitted through forgetfulness, which not having been mentioned in their places, can only be briefly spoken of here;–such as, that my father Bomefree had had two wives before he took Mau-mau Bett; one of whom, if not both, were torn from him by the iron hand of the ruthless trafficker in human flesh;–that my husband, Thomas, after one of his wives had been sold away from him, ran away to New York City, where he remained a year or two, before he was discovered and taken back to the prison-house of slavery;–that my master Dumont, when he promised me one year of my time, before the State should make me free, made the same promise to my husband, and in addition to freedom, we were promised a log cabin for a home of our own; all of which, with the one-thousand-and-one day-dreams resulting there from, went into the repository of unfulfilled promises and unrealized hopes.

When I went to New York City, I went in company with a Miss Grear, who introduced me to the family of Mr. James Latourette, a wealthy merchant, and a Methodist in religion; but who, the latter part of his life, felt that he had outgrown ordinances, and advocated free meetings, holding them at his own dwelling-house for several years previous to his death. I worked for them, and they generously gave me a home while I labored for others, and in their kindness made me as one of their own.

At that time, the 'moral reform' movement was awakening the attention of the benevolent in that city. Many women, among whom were Mrs. Latourette and Miss Grear, became deeply interested in making an attempt to reform their fallen sisters, even the most degraded of them; and in this enterprise of labor and danger, they enlisted me and others, who for a time put forth their most zealous efforts, and performed the work of missionaries with much apparent success. I accompanied those ladies to the most wretched abodes of vice and misery, and sometimes I went where they dared not follow. They even succeeded in establishing prayer-meetings in several places, where such a thing might least have been expected.

But these meetings soon became the most noisy, shouting, ranting, and boisterous of gatherings; where they became delirious with excitement, and then exhausted from over-action. Such meetings I had not much sympathy with, at best. But one evening I attended one of them, where the members of it, in a fit of ecstasy, jumped upon my cloak in such a manner as to drag me to the floor–and then, thinking I had fallen in a spiritual trance, they increased their glorifications on my account,– jumping, shouting, stamping, and clapping of hands; rejoicing so much over my spirit, and so entirely overlooking my body, that I suffered much, both from fear and bruises; and ever after refused to attend any more such meetings, doubting much whether God had any thing to do with such worship.

The Cause of leaving the City

The first years I spent in the city, I accumulated more than enough to satisfy all my wants, and I placed all the overplus in the Savings' Bank. Afterwards, while living with Mr. Pierson, he prevailed on me to take it all out, and invest it in a common fund which he was about establishing, as a fund to be drawn from by all the faithful; the faithful, of course, were the handful that should subscribe to his peculiar creed. This fund, commenced by Mr. Pierson, took my little property and merged it with the rest, where it was dissolved–or went to enrich those who profited by the loss of others, if any such there were. Mr. Pierson and others had so assured me that the fund would supply by and by all my wants, at all times, and in all emergencies, and to the end of life. I believe them and became perfectly careless on the subject–asking for no interest when I drew my money from the bank, and taking no account of the sum I placed in the fund. With this security, I continued my labors, in the hope of yet being able to accumulate a sufficiency to make a little home for myself, in my advancing age. With this stimulus before me, I toiled hard, working early and late, doing a great deal for a little money, and turning my hand to almost anything that promised good pay. Still, I did not prosper, and somehow, could not contrive to lay by a single dollar for a 'rainy day.'

When this had been the state of my affairs for some time, I suddenly paused, and taking a retrospective view of what had passed, inquired within myself, why it was that, for all my unwearied labors, I had nothing to show; why it was that others, with much less care and labor, could hoard up treasures for themselves and children? I became more and more convinced, as I reasoned, that everything I had undertaken in the city of New York had finally proved a failure; and where my hopes had been raised the highest, there I felt the failure had been the greatest, and the disappointment most severe.

After turning it in my mind for some time, I came to the conclusion, that I had been taking part in a great drama, which was, in itself, but one great system of robbery and wrong. 'Yes,' I concluded, 'the rich rob the poor, and the poor rob one another.' True, I had not received labor from others, and stunted their pay, as I felt had been practiced against me; but I had taken their work from them, which was their only means to get money, and was the same to them in the end. For instance–a gentleman where I lived would give me a dollar to hire a poor man to clear the new-fallen snow from the steps and sidewalks. I would arise early, and perform the labor myself, putting the money into my own pocket. A poor man would come along, saying I ought to have let him have the job; he was poor, and needed the pay for his family. I would harden my heart, and answer–'I am poor too, and I need it for mine.' But, in my retrospection, I thought of all the misery I might have been adding to, in my selfish grasping, and it troubled my conscience sorely; and this insensibility to the claims of human brotherhood, and the wants of the destitute and wretched poor, I now see, as I never had done before, to be unfeeling, selfish and wicked.

These reflections and convictions gave rise to a sudden revulsion of feeling in my heart, and I began to look upon money and property with great indifference, if not contempt–being at that time unable, probably, to discern any difference between a miserly grasping at and hoarding of money and means, and a true use of the good things of this life for one's own comfort, and the relief of such as I might be enabled to befriend and assist. One thing I was sure of–that the precepts, 'Do unto others as ye would that others should do unto you,' 'Love your neighbor as yourself,' and so forth, were maxims that had been but little thought of by me, or practiced by those about me.

My next decision was, that I must leave the city; it was no place for me; yea, I felt called in spirit to leave it, and to travel east and lecture. I had never been further east than the city, neither had I any friends there of whom I had particular reason to expect anything; yet to me, it was plain that my mission lay in the east, and that I would find friends there. I determined on leaving; but these determinations and convictions I kept close locked in my own breast, knowing that if my children and friends were aware of it, they would make such an ado about it as would render it very unpleasant, if not distressing to all parties.

Having made what preparations for leaving I deemed necessary,–which was, to put up a few articles of clothing in a pillow-case, all else being deemed an unnecessary incumbrance,–about an hour before I left, I informed Mrs. Whiting, the woman of the house where she was stopping, that my name was no longer Isabella, but SOJOURNER; and that I was going east. And to her inquiry, 'What are you going east for?' my answer was, 'The Spirit calls me there, and I must go.'

I left the city on the morning of the 1st of June, 1843, crossing over to Brooklyn, L.I.; and taking the rising sun for my only compass and guide, I 'remembered Lot's wife,' and hoping to avoid her fate, I resolved not to look back till I felt sure the wicked city from which I was fleeing was left too far behind to be visible in the distance; and when I first ventured to look back, I could just discern the blue cloud of smoke that hung over it, and I thanked the Lord that I was thus far removed from what seemed to me a second Sodom.

I was now fairly started on my pilgrimage; a bundle in one hand, and a little basket of provisions in the other, and two York shillings in my purse–my heart strong in the faith that my true work lay before me, and that the Lord was my director; and I doubted not he would provide for and protect me, and that it would be very censurable to burden myself with anything more than a moderate supply for my then present needs. My mission was not merely to travel east, but to 'lecture,' as I designated it; 'testifying of the hope that was in me'–exhorting the people to embrace Jesus, and refrain from sin, the nature and origin of which I explained to them in accordance with my own most curious and original views.

Wherever night overtook me, there I sought for lodgings–free, if I might–if not, I paid; at a tavern, if I chanced to be at one–if not, at a private dwelling; with the rich, if they would receive me–if not, with the poor.

But I soon discovered that the largest houses were nearly always full; if not quite full, company was soon expected; and that it was much easier to find an unoccupied corner in a small house than in a large one; and if a person possessed but a miserable roof over his head, you might be sure of a welcome to part of it.

But this, I had enough awareness to see, was quite as much the effect of a want of sympathy as of benevolence; and this was also very apparent in my religious conversations with people who were strangers to me. I said, 'I never could find out that the rich had any religion. If I had been rich and accomplished, I could; for the rich could always find religion in the rich, and I could find it among the poor.'

At first, I attended such meetings as I heard of, in the vicinity of my travels, and spoke to the people as I found them assembled. Afterwards, I advertised meetings of my own, and held forth to large audiences, having, as I said, 'a good time.'

When I became weary of traveling, and wished a place to stop a while and rest, some opening was always near at hand; and the first time I needed rest, a man accosted me as I was walking, inquiring if I was looking for work. I told him that was not the object of my travels, but that I would willingly work a few days, if anyone wanted. He requested me to go to his family, who were sadly in want of assistance, which he had been thus far unable to supply. I went to the house where I was directed, and was received by his family, one of whom was ill, as a 'Godsend;' and when I felt constrained to resume my journey, they were very sorry, and would fain have detained me longer; but as I urged the necessity of leaving, they offered me what seemed in my eyes a great deal of money as a remuneration for my labor, and an expression of their gratitude for my opportune assistance; but I would only receive a very little of it; enough, as I say, to enable me to pay tribute to Caesar, if it was demanded of me; and two or three York shillings at a time were all I allowed myself to take; and then, with purse replenished, and strength renewed, I would once more set out to perform my mission.

Travel Tribulations

As I drew near the centre of the Island, I commenced, one evening at nightfall, to solicit the favor of a night's lodging. I had repeated my request a great many, it seemed to me some twenty times, and as many times I received a negative answer. I walked on, the stars and the tiny horns of the new moon shed but a dim light on my lonely way, when I was familiarly accosted by two Indians, who took me for an acquaintance. I told them they were mistaken in the person; I was a stranger there, and asked them the direction to a tavern. They informed me it was yet a long way–some two miles or so; and inquired if I were alone. Not wishing for their protection, or knowing what might be the character of their kindness, I answered, 'No, not exactly,' and passed on.

At the end of a weary way, I came to the tavern,–or rather, to a large building, which was occupied as a court-house, tavern, and jail,–and on asking for a night's lodging, was informed I could stay, if I would consent to be locked in. This to my mind was an insuperable objection. To have a key turned on me was a thing not to be thought of, at least not to be endured, and I again took up my line of march, preferring to walk beneath the open sky, to being locked up by a stranger in such a place. I had not walked far, before I heard the voice of a woman under an open shed; I ventured to accost her, and inquired if she knew where I could get in for the night. The woman answered that she did not, unless I went home with them; and turning to her 'good man,' asked him if the stranger could share their home for the night, to which he cheerfully assented. I thought it evident he had been taking a drop too much, but as he was civil and good-natured, and I did not feel inclined to spend the night alone in the open air, I felt driven to the necessity of accepting their hospitality, whatever it might prove to be. The woman soon informed me that there was a ball in the place, at which they would like to drop in a while, before they went to their home.

Balls have never been part of my mission, therefore I was not desirous of attending; but my hostess could be satisfied with nothing short of a taste of it, and I was forced to go with her, or relinquish their company at once, in which move there might be more exposure than in accompanying her. I went, and soon found myself surrounded by an assemblage of people, collected from the very dregs of society, too ignorant and degraded to understand, much less entertain, a high or bright idea,–in a dirty hovel, destitute of every comfort, and where the fumes of whiskey were abundant and powerful.

My guide there was too much charmed with the combined entertainments of the place to be able to tear herself away, till she found her faculties for enjoyment failing her, from a too free use of liquor; and she betook herself to bed till she could recover them. I, seated in a corner, had time for many reflections, and refrained from lecturing them, in obedience to the recommendation, 'Cast not your pearls,' etc.

When the night was far spent, the husband of the sleeping woman aroused the sleeper, and reminded her that she was not very polite to the woman she had invited to sleep at her house, and of the propriety of returning home. They once more emerged into the pure air, which to me, after so long breathing the noisome air of the ballroom, was most refreshing and grateful. Just as day dawned, they reached the place they called their home. I now saw that I had lost nothing in the shape of rest by remaining so long at the ball, as their miserable cabin afforded but one bunk or pallet for sleeping; and had there been many such, I would have preferred sitting up all night to occupying one like it.

They very politely offered me the bed, if I would use it; but civilly declining, I waited for morning with an eagerness of desire I never felt before on the subject, and was never more happy than when the eye of day shed its golden light once more over the earth. I was once more free, and while daylight should last, independent, and needed no invitation to pursue my journey. Let these facts teach us, that every pedestrian in the world is not a vagabond, and that it is a dangerous thing to compel anyone to receive hospitality—as thousands can testify, who have thus been caught in the snares of the wicked.

I arrived at Huntingdon on the fourth of July; from thence I went to Cold Springs, where I found the people making preparations for a mass temperance-meeting. With my usual alacrity, I joined their labors, getting up dishes a la New York, greatly to the satisfaction of those I assisted. After remaining at Cold Springs some three weeks, I returned to Huntingdon, where I took a boat for Connecticut. Landing at Bridgeport, I again resumed my travels towards the north-east, lecturing some, and working some, to get enough to pay tribute to Caesar, as I called it; and in this manner I presently came to the city of New Haven, where I found many meetings, which I attended—at some of which, I was allowed to express my views freely, and without reservation. I also called meetings expressly to give myself an opportunity to be heard; and found in the city many true friends of Jesus, with whom I held communion of spirit, having no preference for one sect more than another, but being well satisfied with all who gave me evidence of having known or loved the Saviour.

After thus delivering my testimony in this pleasant city, feeling I had not as yet found an abiding place, I went from there to Bristol, at the request of a zealous sister, who desired me to go to the latter place, and hold a conversation with some friends of hers there. I went as requested, found the people kind and through them I became acquainted with several very interesting persons.

A spiritually-minded brother in Bristol, becoming interested in my new views and original opinions, requested as a favor that I would go to Hartford, to see and converse with friends of his there. Standing ready to perform any service in the Lord, I went to Hartford as desired, bearing in my hand the following note from this brother:–

'SISTER,–I send you this living messenger, as I believe her to be one that God loves. You can see by this sister, that God does by his Spirit alone teach his own children things to come. Please receive her, and she will tell you some new things. Let her tell her story without interrupting her, and give close attention, and you will see she has got the lever of truth, that God helps her to pry where but few can.
Send her to brother, and where she can do the most good.
From your brother, H. L. B.'

Some of my views

As soon as I saw God as an all-powerful, all-pervading spirit, I became desirous of hearing all that had been written of him, and listened to the account of the creation of the world and its first inhabitants, as contained in the first chapters of Genesis, with peculiar interest. For some time I received it all literally, though it appeared strange to me that 'God worked by the day, got tired, and stopped to rest,' etc. But after a little time, she began to reason upon it, thus–'Why, if God works by the day, and one day's work tires him, and he is obliged to rest, either from weariness or on account of darkness, or if he waited for the "cool of the day to walk in the garden," because he was inconvenienced by the heat of the sun, why then it seems that God cannot do as much as I can; for I can bear the sun at noon, and work several days and nights in succession without being much tired. Or, if he rested nights because of the darkness, it is very queer that he should make the night so dark that he could not see himself. If I had been God, I would have made the night light enough for my own convenience, surely.'

But the moment I placed this idea of God by the side of the impression I had once so suddenly received of his inconceivable greatness and entire spirituality, that moment I exclaimed mentally, 'No, God does not stop to rest, for he is a spirit, and cannot tire; he cannot want for light, for he hath all light in himself. And if "God is all in all," and "worketh all in all," as I have heard them read, then it is impossible he should rest at all; for if he did, every other thing would stop and rest too; the waters would not flow, and the fishes could not swim; and all motion must cease. God could have no pauses in his work, and he needed no Sabbaths of rest. Man might need them, and he should take them when he needed them, whenever he required rest. As it regarded the worship of God, he was to be worshipped at all times and in all places; and one portion of time never seemed to her more holy than another.'

These views, which were the results of the workings of my own mind, assisted solely by the light of my own experience and very limited knowledge, were, for a long time after their adoption, closely locked in my own breast, fearing that their avowal might bring me the imputation of 'infidelity,'–the usual charge preferred by all religionists, against those who entertain religious views and feelings differing materially from their own.

While traveling in Connecticut, I met a minister, with whom I held a long discussion on these points, as well as on various other topics, such as the origin of all things, especially the origin of evil, at the same time bearing my testimony strongly against a paid ministry. He belonged to that class, and, as a matter of course, as strongly advocated his own side of the question.

I had forgotten to mention, in its proper place, a very important fact, that when I was examining the Scriptures, I wished to hear them without comment; but if I employed adult persons to read them to me, (since I didn't know how to read) and asked them to read a passage over again, they invariably commenced to explain, by giving me their version of it; and in this way, they tried my feelings exceedingly. In consequence of this, I ceased to ask adult persons to read the Bible to me, and substituted children in their stead. Children, as soon as they could read distinctly, would re-read the same sentence to me, as often as I wished, and without comment; and in that way I was enabled to see what my own mind could make out of the record, and that was what I wanted, and not what others thought it to mean. I wished to compare the teachings of the Bible with what I had witness; and I came to the conclusion, that the spirit of truth spoke in those records, but that the recorders of those truths had intermingled with them ideas and suppositions of their own. Once I liberated myself from all my earthly masters, I only served my one and only Master, God.

When it became known to my children, that I had left New York, they were filled with wonder and alarm. Where could I have gone, and why had I left? were questions no one could answer satisfactorily. Now, their imaginations painted me as a wandering maniac–and again they feared I had been left for death; and many were the tears they shed at the loss of me.

But when I reached Berlin, Conn., I wrote to them by amanuensis, informing them of my whereabouts, and waiting an answer to my letter; thus quieting their fears, and gladdening their hearts once more with assurances of my continued life and my love.

Camp meeting

I had been at Northampton a few months, when I attended a camp-meeting, at which I performed a very important part.

A party of wild young men, with no motive but that of entertaining themselves by annoying and injuring the feelings of others, had assembled at the meeting, hooting and yelling, and in various ways interrupting the services, and causing much disturbance. Those who had the charge of the meeting, having tried their persuasive powers in vain, grew impatient and tried threatening.

The young men, considering themselves insulted, collected their friends, to the number of a hundred or more, dispersed themselves through the grounds, making the most frightful noises, and threatening to fire the tents. It was said the authorities of the meeting sat in grave consultation, decided to have the ring-leaders arrested, and sent for the constable, to the great displeasure of some of the company, who were opposed to such an appeal to force and arms. Be that as it may, I, seeing great consternation depicted in every countenance, caught the contagion, and, before I was aware, I found myself quaking with fear.

Under the impulse of this sudden emotion, I fled to the most retired corner of a tent, and secreted myself behind a trunk. saying to myself, 'I am the only colored person here, and on me, probably, their wicked mischief will fall first, and perhaps fatally.' But feeling how great was my insecurity even there, as the very tent began to shake from its foundations, I began to soliloquize as follows:–

'Shall I run away and hide from the Devil? Me, a servant of the living God? Have I not faith enough to go out and quell that mob, when I know it is written–"One shall chase a thousand, and two put ten thousand to flight"? I know there are not a thousand here; and I know I am a servant of the living God. I'll go to the rescue, and the Lord shall go with and protect me.

Oh, after that, I felt as if I had three hearts! and that they were so large, my body could hardly hold them!

I now came forth from my hiding-place, and invited several to go with me and see what they could do to still the raging fellows. They declined, and considered me wild to think of it.

The meeting was in the open fields–the full moon shed its saddened light overall–and the woman who was that evening to address them was trembling on the preachers' stand. The noise and confusion were now terrific. I left the tent alone and unaided, and walking some thirty rods to the top of a small rise of ground, commenced to sing, in my most fervid manner, with all the strength of my most powerful voice, the hymn on the resurrection of Christ–

It was early in the morning–it was early in the morning,
Just at the break of day–
When he rose–when he rose–when he rose,
And went to heaven on a cloud.'

As I commenced to sing, the young men made a rush toward me, and I was immediately encircled by a dense body of the rioters, many of them armed with sticks or clubs as their weapons of defense, if not of attack. As the circle narrowed around me, I ceased singing, and after a short pause, inquired, in a gentle but firm tone, 'Why do you come about me with clubs and sticks? I am not doing harm to any one.'

'We ar'n't a going to hurt you, old woman; we came to hear you sing,' cried many voices, simultaneously. 'Sing to us, old woman,' cried one. 'Talk to us, old woman,' said another. 'Pray, old woman,' said a third. 'Tell us your experience,' said a fourth. 'You stand and smoke so near me, I cannot sing or talk,' I answered.

'Stand back,' said several authoritative voices, with not the most gentle or courteous accompaniments, raising their rude weapons in the air.

The crowd suddenly gave back, the circle became larger, as many voices again called for singing, talking, or praying, backed by assurances that no one should be allowed to hurt me–the speakers declaring with an oath, that they would 'knock down' any person who should offer me the least indignity.

I looked about me, and started to speak; they silently heard, and civilly asked me many questions. They gave me time to answer them with truth and they thought I was speaking wisdom that was beyond myself. My speech operated on their roused passions like oil on agitated waters; they were, as a whole, entirely subdued, and only clamored when I ceased to speak or sing. Those who stood in the background, after the circle was enlarged, cried out, 'Sing aloud, old woman, we can't hear.' Those who held the scepter of power among them requested that she should make a pulpit of a neighboring wagon.

I said, 'If I do, they'll overthrow it.'
'No, they shan't–he who dares hurt you, we'll knock him down instantly, d–n him,' cried the chiefs. 'No we won't, no we won't, nobody shall hurt you,' answered the many voices of the mob.

They kindly assisted me to mount the wagon, from which I spoke and sung to them about an hour. Of all I said to them on the occasion, I remember only the following:–
'Well, there are two congregations on this ground. It is written that there shall be a separation, and the sheep shall be separated from the goats. The other preachers have the sheep, I have the goats. And I have a few sheep among my goats, but they are very ragged.'

This exordium produced great laughter. When I became wearied with talking, I began to cast about me to contrive some way to induce them to disperse. While I paused, they loudly clamored for 'more,' 'more,'–'sing,' 'sing more.' I motioned them to be quiet, and called out to them:

'Children, I have talked and sung to you, as you asked me; and now I have a request to make of you; will you grant it?'

'Yes, yes, yes,' resounded from every quarter.

'Well, it is this,' I answered; 'if I will sing one more hymn for you, will you then go away, and leave us this night in peace?'

'Yes, yes,' came faintly, feebly from a few.

'I'll ask you again and I want an answer from you all, as of one accord. If I will sing you one more, will you go away, and leave us this night in peace?'

'Yes, yes, yes,' shouted many voices, with hearty emphasis.

'I repeat my request once more,' I said, 'and I want you ALL to answer.'

And I reiterated the words again. This time a long, loud 'Yes–yes–yes,' came up, as from the multitudinous mouth of the entire mob.

'AMEN! it is SEALED,' I repeated, in the deepest and most solemn tones of my powerful and sonorous voice. Its effect ran through the multitude, like an electric shock; and most of them considered themselves bound by their promise, as they might have failed to do under less imposing circumstances. Some of them began instantly to leave; others said, 'Are we not to have one more hymn?'

'Yes,' I answered, and I commenced to sing:

'I bless the Lord I've got my seal–today and today–
To slay Goliath in the field–today and today;
The good old way is a righteous way,
I mean to take the kingdom in the good old way.'

While singing, I heard some enforcing obedience to their promise, while a few seemed refusing to abide by it. But before I had quite concluded, I saw them turn from me, and in the course of a few minutes, they were running as fast as they well could in a solid body. To me, they look like nothing but a swarm of bees, so dense was their phalanx, so straight their course, so hurried their march. As they passed with a rush very near the stand of the other preachers, the hearts of the people were smitten with fear, thinking that their entertainer had failed to enchain them longer with her spell, and that they were coming upon them with redoubled and remorseless fury. But they found they were mistaken, and that their fears were groundless; for, before they could well recover from their surprise, every rioter was gone, and not one was left on the grounds, or seen there again during the meeting. I was informed that as her audience reached the main road, some distance from the tents, a few of the rebellious spirits refused to go on, and proposed returning; but their leaders said, 'No–we have promised to leave–

all promised, and we must go, all go, and you shall none of you return again.'

I did not fall in love at first sight with the Northampton Association, for I arrived there at a time when appearances did not correspond with the ideas of associationists, as they had been spread out in their writings; for their phalanx was a factory, and they were wanting in means to carry out their ideas of beauty and elegance, as they would have done in different circumstances. But I thought I would make an effort to tarry with them one night, though that seemed to me no desirable affair. But as soon as I saw that accomplished, literary, and refined persons were living in that plain and simple manner, and submitting to the labors and privations incident to such an infant institution, I said, 'Well, if these can live here, I can.'

Afterwards, I gradually became pleased with, and attached to, the place and the people, as well as I could; for it was not a small thing to have found a home in a 'Community composed of some of the choicest spirits of the age,' where all was characterized by an equality of feeling, a liberty of thought and speech, and a largeness of soul, people I could not have before met with, to the same extent, in any of my wanderings.

I had now set my heart upon having a little home of my own, even at this late hour of life, where I may feel a greater freedom than I can in the house of another, and where I can repose a little, after my day of action has passed by. And for such a 'home' I am now dependent on the charities of the benevolent, and to them, I appeal with confidence.

With all my fervor, and enthusiasm, and speculation, my faith is not tinctured in the least with gloom. No doubt, no hesitation, no despondency, spreads a cloud over my soul; but all is bright, clear, positive, and at times ecstatic. My trust is in God, and from him, I look for good, and not evil. I feel that 'perfect love casteth out fear.'

My last interview with my master

In the spring of 1849, I made a visit to my eldest daughter, Diana, who has ever suffered from ill health, and remained with Mr. Dumont, my former master. I found him still living, though advanced in age, and reduced in property, (as he had been for a number of years,) but greatly enlightened on the subject of slavery. He said he could then see that 'slavery was the wickedest thing in the world, the greatest curse the earth had ever felt–that it was then very clear to his mind that it was so, though, while he was a slaveholder himself, he did not see it so, and thought it was as right as holding any other property.' I remarked to him, that it might be the same with those who are now slaveholders.

'O, no,' replied he, with warmth, 'it cannot be. For, now, the sin of slavery is so clearly written out, and so much talked against,–(why, the whole world cries out against it!)–that if anyone says he doesn't know, and has not heard, he must, I think, be a liar. In my slaveholding days, there were few that spoke against it, and these few made little impression on anyone. Had it been as it is now, think you I could have held slaves? No! I should not have dared to do it, but should have emancipated every one of them. Now, it is very different; all may hear if they will.'

Yes, reader, if anyone feels that the tocsin of alarm, or the anti-slavery trump, must sound a louder note before they can hear it, one would think they must be very hard of hearing,–yea, that they belong to that class, of whom it may be truly said, 'they have stopped their ears that they may not hear.'

I received a letter from my daughter Diana, dated Hyde Park, December 19, 1849, which informed me that Mr. Dumont had 'gone West' with some of his sons–that he had taken along with him, probably through mistake, the few articles of furniture I had left with him.

'Never mind,' I said, 'what we give to the poor, we lend to the Lord.'

And I thanked the Lord with fervor, that I had lived to hear my master say such blessed things! I recalled the lectures he used to give his slaves, on speaking the truth and being honest, and laughing, I recalled he taught us not to lie and steal, when he was stealing all the time himself, and did not know it! Oh! how sweet to my mind was this confession! And what a confession for a master to make to a slave! A slaveholding master turned to a brother! Poor old man, may the Lord bless him, and all slaveholders partake of his spirit!

END OF THE NARRATIVE.

Appendix - Certificates of character

HURLEY, ULSTER Co., Oct. 13th, 1834

This is to certify, that I am well acquainted with Isabella, this colored woman; I have been acquainted with her from her infancy; she has been in my employ for one year, and she was a faithful servant, honest, and industrious; and have always known her to be in good report by all who employed her.

ISAAC S. VAN WAGENEN. NEW PALTZ, ULSTER Co., Oct. 13th, 1834

This is to certify, that Isabella, this colored woman, lived with me since the year 1810, and that she has always been a good and faithful servant; and the eighteen years that she was with me, I always found her to be perfectly honest. I have always heard her well spoken of by everyone that has employed her.

JOHN J. DUMONT

NORTHAMPTON, March 1850

We, the undersigned having known Isabella (or Sojourner Truth) for several years, most cheerfully bear testimony to her uniform good character, her untiring industry, kind deportment, unwearied benevolence, and the many social and excellent traits which make her worthy to bear her adopted name.

Note from the Olive Gilbert, to whom Sojourner Truth originally dictated her story.

O the 'fantastic tricks' which the American people are 'playing before high Heaven!' O their profane use of the sacred name of Liberty! O their impious appeal to the God of the oppressed, for his divine benediction while they are making merchandise of his image! Do they not blush? Nay, they glory in their shame! Once a year they take special pains to exhibit themselves to the world in all their republican deformity and Christian barbarity, insanely supposing that they thus excite the envy, admiration and applause of mankind. The nations are looking at the dreadful spectacle with disgust and amazement. However sunken and degraded they may be, they are too elevated, too virtuous, too humane to be guilty of such conduct. Their voice is heard, saying–'Americans! we hear your boasts of liberty, your shouts of independence, your declarations of hostility to every form of tyranny, your assertions that all men are created free and equal, and endowed by their Creator with an inalienable right to liberty, the merry peal of your bells, and the deafening roar of your artillery; but, mingling with all these, and rising above them all, we also hear the clanking of chains! the shrieks and wailings of millions of your own countrymen, whom you wickedly hold in a state of slavery as much more frightful than the oppression which your fathers resisted unto blood, as the tortures of the Inquisition surpass the stings of an insect! We see your banner floating proudly in the breeze from every flag-staff and mast-head in the land; but its blood-red stripes are emblematical of your own slave-driving cruelty, as you apply the lash to the flesh of your guiltless victim, even the flesh of a wife and mother, shrieking for the restoration of the babe of her bosom, sold to the remorseless slave speculator! We catch the gleam of your illuminated hills, everywhere blazing with bonfires; we mark your cheerful processions; we note the number of your orators; we listen to the recital of your revolutionary achievements; we see you kneeling at the shrine of Freedom, as her best, her truest, her sincerest worshippers! Shouldn't it be considered an hypocrisy? Professing to believe in the natural equality of the human race–yet dooming a sixth portion of your immense population to beastly servitude, and ranking them among your goods and chattels! Boasting of your democracy–yet determining the rights of men by the texture of their hair and the color of their skin! Assuming to be 'the land of the free and the home of the brave,–yet keeping in chains more slaves than any other nation, not excepting slave-cursed Brazil! Prating of your morality and honesty–yet denying the rites of marriage to three millions of human beings, and plundering them of all their hard earnings! Affecting to be horror-struck in view of the foreign slave-trade–yet eagerly pursuing a domestic traffic equally cruel and unnatural, and reducing to slavery not less than seventy thousand new victims annually! Vaunting of your freedom of speech and of the press–your matchless Constitution and your glorious Union–yet denouncing as traitors, and treating as outlaws, those who have the courage and fidelity to plead for immediate, untrammeled, universal emancipation! Monsters that ye are! how can ye expect to escape the scorn of the world, and the wrath of Heaven? Emancipate your slaves, if you would redeem your tarnished character–if you would obtain forgiveness here, and salvation hereafter! Until you do so, "there will be a stain upon your national escutcheon, which all the waters of the Atlantic cannot wash out!"'

It is hoped that the perusal of the following Narrative may increase the sympathy that is felt for the suffering colored population of this country, and inspire to renewed efforts for the liberation of all who are pining in bondage on the American soil.

- Olive Gilbert, 1850

DON'T MISS THE REST OF THE SERIES

VOICES OF FREEDOM

AT PADMORE CULTURE.COM

www.ingramcontent.com/pod-product-compliance
Lightning Source LLC
Chambersburg PA
CBHW071517080526
44588CB00011B/1463